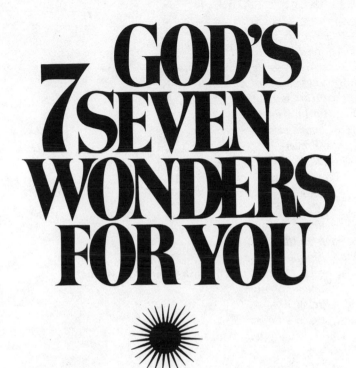

# 7 GOD'S SEVEN WONDERS FOR YOU

# BY CHARLES L. ALLEN

God's Psychiatry
The Touch of the Master's Hand
All Things Are Possible Through Prayer
When You Lose a Loved One
When the Heart Is Hungry
The Twenty-third Psalm
The Ten Commandments
The Lord's Prayer
The Beatitudes
Twelve Ways to Solve Your Problems
Healing Words
The Life of Christ
Prayer Changes Things
The Sermon on the Mount
Life More Abundant
The Charles L. Allen Treasury (with Charles L. Wallis)
Roads to Radiant Living
Riches of Prayer
In Quest of God's Power
When You Graduate (with Mouzon Biggs)
The Miracle of Love
The Miracle of Hope
The Miracle of the Holy Spirit
Christmas in Our Hearts (with Charles L. Wallis)
Candle, Star and Christmas Tree (with Charles L. Wallis)
When Christmas Came to Bethlehem (with Charles L. Wallis)
Christmas (with Charles L. Wallis)
What I Have Lived By
You Are Never Alone
Perfect Peace
How to Increase Your Sunday-School Attendance (with Mildred Parker)
The Secret of Abundant Living
Victory in the Valleys of Life
Faith, Hope, and Love
Joyful Living
Inspiring Thoughts for Your Marriage
When a Marriage Ends
God's Seven Wonders for You

# 7 GOD'S SEVEN WONDERS FOR YOU

## Charles L. Allen

FLEMING H. REVELL COMPANY
OLD TAPPAN, NEW JERSEY

Unless otherwise identified, Scripture quotations are from the King James Version of the Bible.

Scripture quotations identified RSV are from the Revised Standard Version of the Bible, copyrighted © 1946, 1952, 1971, by the Division of Christian Education of the National Council of Churches of Christ in the United States of America, and are used by permission.

Scripture quotations identified MOFFATT are from THE BIBLE: A NEW TRANSLATION by James Moffatt. Copyright 1926 by Harper & Row Publishers, Inc., renewed 1954 by James A. R. Moffatt. Reprinted by permission of the publishers.

Scripture quotations identified RV are from the Revised Version of the Bible.

Permission to quote from the following is gratefully acknowledged:

Quotation from THE PROPHET by Kahlil Gibran reprinted by permission of Alfred A. Knopf, Inc. Copyright 1923 by Kahlil Gibran and renewed 1951 by Administrators C.T.A. of Kahlil Gibran Estate and Mary G. Gibran.

"Sermons We See" reprinted from THE COLLECTED VERSE OF EDGAR A. GUEST, © 1934 by Contemporary Books, Inc., used with permission.

"Have You Come to the Red Sea Place in Your Life?" by Annie Johnson Flint, used by permission of Evangelical Publishers, a division of Scripture Press Publications, Ltd., Whitby, Ontario.

**Library of Congress Cataloging-in-Publication Data**

Allen, Charles Livingstone, 1913–
    God's seven wonders for you.

    1. Christian Life—Methodist authors.
I. Title.
BV4501.2.A396    1987        234        87-28504
ISBN 0-8007-1565-9

# Contents

I dedicate this book to my children and grandchildren
who I love very, very much:

*Charles L. Allen, Jr.*
*Lorraine Lee Allen*
*Charles L. Allen, III*
*Karina Sellers Allen*
*Margaret Ann Allen*
*Jack deMange Allen*

*John Franklin Allen*
*Ann Woolsey Allen*
*John Franklin Allen, Jr.*
*Benson Haynes Allen*
*Meredith Ann Allen*

*Charles W. Miller*
*Mary Jane Allen Miller*
*Charles W. (Chuck) Miller, Jr.*
*Carolyn Kay (Carrie) Miller*
*John O'Brien Miller*

# Introduction

# The Seven Ancient Wonders

A young man came into my office to ask if I would help him write a paper on the seven wonders of the ancient world. I was delighted to help him and I suggested we first list them.

I said pyramids—and he wrote that one down. Then I could not think of another one. I said, "Instead of me telling you about them, let's go downstairs to the library and read about them." That we did and it was a thrilling experience. Those ancient wonders were indeed wonderful—they are:

1. The Pyramids of Egypt, built as tombs for Egyptian kings, are the oldest and best preserved of all the ancient wonders.
2. The Hanging Gardens of Babylon were built by King Nebuchadnezzar II for one of his wives.
3. The Temple of Artemis of Ephesus, built about 550 B.C., one of the largest and most complicated temples built in ancient times.
4. The Statue of Zeus at Olympia, Greece, considered to be the most famous statue in the ancient world.
5. The Mausoleum at Halicarnassus, in Southwestern Turkey, a huge marble building built as a tomb for Mausolus.
6. The Colossus of Rhodes was a huge bronze statue that stood near the harbor of Rhodes on the Aegean Sea.
7. The Lighthouse of Alexandria, about 440 feet high, stood on the island of Pharos in the harbor of Alexandria, Egypt.

After he was gone, I sat thinking about those wonders. Then I began to think of some of the wonders of our world today—the miracle of creation, the birth of a baby, and so many wonderful things which have happened.

I thought of Niagara Falls, the Grand Canyon, and many other places we like to visit. I thought of airplanes and television and so many things which have been created. Truly we live in a world filled with wonders.

Then I thought of the most wonderful wonders of all—the wonders of the spiritual world—and those are the wonders this book is about.

In every sermon I ever preached and in every book I have written, some of these seven spiritual wonders have been included. So, to anyone who has heard my sermons or read my books, these pages may seem familiar, yet they are still thrilling.

CHARLES L. ALLEN
5100 SAN FELIPE #182
HOUSTON, TEXAS 77056

# 1

## *The First Spiritual Wonder:*

## God's Love for You

 When someone asked me to preach on "Why I Believe in God," I thought it would be easy to do. Quickly I can think of a dozen reasons to believe in God, but as I look at those reasons, I know they are not my reasons. My books on theology give the arguments for God and studying those books has strengthened my faith and confirmed my beliefs. But it would not be honest for me to copy the reasons for belief in God from my books and give them as my own.

The fact is, I believed in God before I ever studied theology. The more I think about it, the more I realize that I believed before I knew the reasons. I know now that it is necessary for me to breathe and that without air I would die. But long before I knew that, I just breathed.

I was born into a home where prayer was heard regularly. I did not question that there was a God to hear those prayers. I just accepted the fact. I was taken to church, and it has always seemed normal and right for me to belong to the church. Long before I knew how the church came to be, or the reasons for its existence, I felt at home in it. I am a Christian, and day by day, as I learn more about Christ, I love Him more and I praise Him more for the salvation of my soul. For years I have given my life to the ministry and I am sure that is what I was meant to do. But I do not remember when I decided for the ministry. I never thought of doing anything else. I think God created me for that purpose and put it into my mind at birth.

In an American court of law, a person is presumed innocent until he is proven guilty. So it is with my own belief in God. Instead of saying I will not believe until God's existence is proved, I have believed and I will continue to believe, until it is proven that there is no God. I have never had any cause to doubt the existence of God; thus I have never felt the necessity of trying to prove Him.

The Bible feels no necessity for proving God; it assumes God's existence. The Bible's very first words are: "In the beginning God . . ." and it goes on to give us a progressive revelation of God. Moses teaches us the laws of God; the Psalms lead us to communion with Him; Micah tells us of His ethical standards; Christ gives us the full revelation of the Father.

Jesus said to His disciples, "Let not your heart be troubled: ye believe in God . . ." (John 14:1). He did not say, "If you believe," or "You should believe." He simply said, "Ye believe" and went on to tell of the Father's house and the way to it.

God does not depend on reasons or arguments for our belief in Him. God took care of that in our creation. Call it instinct, insight, intuition, or any other name, we were born believing that God exists. As we study and learn, as we live and experience, our belief can be strengthened and enlarged. Or our belief can be perverted and misdirected. Therein lies the danger. The Ten Commandments do not command us to believe, but they do command us to keep God as the first object of our worship.

One does not need to understand God in order to believe in Him. The fact is, we understand very few things that we do. In his book, *Nature of the Physical World,* Dr. Arthur Eddington wrote:

I am standing on the threshold about to enter a room. It is a complicated business. In the first place, I must shove against an atmosphere pressing with a force of fourteen pounds on every square inch of my body. I must make sure of landing on a plank traveling at twenty miles a second round the sun. I must do this while hanging from a round planet, head outward into space.

Only a few scientists, like Dr. Eddington, bother to understand what is involved in the process of walking into a room. The rest of us just walk in.

Most of us do not understand the composition of water, but we drink it. None of us know what electricity is, but we use it. Who can understand the process of love? Yet many have given their lives in sacrifice because they loved. Though we cannot explain God, most of us say with Christopher Morley: "I had a thousand questions to ask God; but when I met Him, they all fled and didn't seem to matter."

To say, "I believe in God," means more than just an intellectual assent to the existence of God. It means to trust in Him and to commit our lives to His will. I know a man who was suffering with severe headaches. He went to the doctor and his case was diagnosed as a tumor on the brain. The man had no way of knowing whether or not the doctor was correct. He had to have faith in him.

Because he had faith in the doctor, the man permitted himself to be put to sleep in a room where none of his family or friends were. He gave his consent for the doctor to open his head and cut into his brain. One slip of the knife by just one tiny fraction of an inch would have meant instant death to the patient, yet he was willing to have the operation. His belief in the doctor meant he was willing and ready to trust himself to the doctor's hands.

We trust in God because we realize our own weaknesses and inadequacies. As long as we feel sufficient unto ourselves, we do not need God; we are our own god. No person ever really finds God until there is a felt need in his life that only God can fill. Until you need Him, you won't have Him.

We sometimes say it is our duty to go to church, and it is; but very few go for that reason. I would prefer that no one come to my church out of a sense of duty. The ones who gain the most from church are those who come out of a sense of need. Their minds are open to the truth of God, and their hearts are open to the presence of God. The person who comes to church really seeking God will be impressed by the very existence of the church building.

During the singing of the hymns at church, I see many people who inspire me. They have problems and burdens, but they have something else which enables them to sing. During the time of prayer, I am impressed with the fact that so many really do pray. Surely there must be something to it.

A young lady talked to me about a job in the church. I asked her what salary she expected, and she told me that salary did not matter. She said, "I will live on whatever I get. What I want is the opportunity to serve God."

She inspired me, as does the memory of those who, down through the centuries, have made large sacrifices for their faith. As the minister reads from the Bible and talks about it, I realize there must be a reason why this Book outlasts all other books. These and other thoughts inspire my spirit, lift my confidence, and make me surer of God.

On the other hand, if one comes to church without a sense of need, he is likely to have a cynical spirit. He finds fault with the building, he looks at the people around him and criticizes them, he doubts the sincerity of the minister, he thinks the choir is trying to show off. That person came for nothing and he receives nothing—better for him to have stayed at home.

We never really believe in God until we feel the need for Him. As Giles Fletcher put it in his poem "The Excellency of Christ":

> He is a path, if any be misled;
> He is a robe, if any naked be;
> If any chance to hunger, he is bread;
> If any be a bondman, he is free;
> If any be but weak, how strong is he!
> To dead men, life is he; to sick men, health;
> To blind men, sight; and to the needy, wealth;
> A pleasure without loss, a treasure without stealth.

## How to Believe in God

"Please tell me how I can believe in God," a friend of mine requested. This friend went on to say, "You talk about God as if everybody knew Him. But I don't know who He is, where He is, or what He does. As far as I know, I have never had any conscious dealing with God. In your sermons you say, 'Put your life in God's hands and He will carry you through.' That is like saying to one who has never flown a plane, 'Get into that jet and fly it wherever you want to go.' I do not doubt the plane's existence or its ability to carry me, but I do know I cannot fly it. As for God, I am not even sure that He exists, and certainly I do not know how to 'put myself in His hands.' "

In seeking a plain and straightforward answer, I turned to the ninth chapter of Mark's Gospel and read it carefully. Jesus and three of His disciples went up on the mountain and there had a marvelous experience. Before the eyes of the disciples Jesus' raiment became shining; He was transfigured before them. Then Elijah and Moses suddenly appeared and they talked together. It was so wonderful that Peter suggested they just stay on the mountain. But Jesus knew there was work to be done in the valley below. God never gives His power to those who will not use it in service. At the foot of the mountain was a father who had brought his epileptic son. Since childhood, the boy had been afflicted. The father had asked the disciples to heal the boy but they could not. Now he asked Jesus.

Jesus said, "If thou canst believe, all things are possible to him that believeth" (Mark 9:23). Let's stop on that word "believe." What do we mean by it? "Believe" is used in at least three different senses. A person can say, "I believe in the North Pole." He may not have been there, but he accepts the authority of one who has been there and knows that it exists. Another says, "I believe that two times two is four." That is something he can reason out for himself. Thus his belief is based on his own intellect. Another says, "I believe the sunshine is warm." He has been in the sunshine and felt it; thus his belief is based on experience. Maybe he cannot explain why the sunshine is warm, but he knows it is.

There are many who sincerely want to believe in God but find it hard. Faith never comes easy, and the only way it can come is by beginning wherever we can and then going on from there. No one believes in all of God. No one can. God is so great and we are so small that we can only believe in a part of Him. A man once said to Jesus, "Lord, I believe; help thou mine unbelief" (Mark 9:24). No person believes completely.

The other day I stood on the beach by the ocean. The water lay before me, as far as I could see. I could feel it, I could taste the salt in it, I could swim in it and be carried by the waves. I believe in the ocean because I have seen it and I have felt it. But I do not know the whole sea. I have not been with Admiral Byrd into the Arctic and Antarctic; I have not been into the tropic ocean where the mighty Amazon pours its floods out so freely.

In the ocean there are mountain ranges higher and longer than any man has ever seen. There are canyons in the ocean deeper than any upon dry earth. There is a lot of land area on the earth, but the sea is more than twice as large. Any man could spend his entire life studying the sea and know only a small part of it.

Although we do not know it all, we can still say with assurance, "I believe in the sea."

I can say I believe in people, yet I base the belief on a very limited acquaintance. My immediate family I know intimately. I have some very close friends, and as I go about, I meet what seems to me a lot of people. I have met as many as a thousand people in one week. Yet if all the people I have ever seen face to face were put together, they would represent only a very small part of the billions of people of the world. In the people I do know, however, I have seen love and faith, loyalty and unselfishness, goodness and integrity, to the extent that I do believe in people. I do not have to know every person before I learn to believe.

So I believe in God; He is so great that I can never know Him, yet He is so near that I cannot help but know Him. The Bible tells us "God is love" (1 John 4:8). I have loved and I have been loved. I have seen love expressed in many ways. Seeing and feeling love, I have come to believe in it. Believing in love is believing in God— a small part of God, to be sure, but still God.

Each day we can know a little more of God. We can never know all of Him, but instead of worrying about the part of God I do not know, I say, "Lord, I believe; help me to believe more."

## Look at Something Big

Here is one of the grandest verses in the Bible: "When I consider thy heavens, the work of thy fingers, the moon and the stars, which thou hast ordained . . ." (Psalms 8:3).

Have you ever wondered why God made the world so beautiful, so impressive, so big? Nobody knows how big the heavens are with their billions of stars. God didn't have to make it that big in order for the earth to exist. Why did God make it so that every morning the glory of a sunrise would come over the earth and every evening the quiet beauty of a sunset? He could have arranged it so the day would come and go in some less impressive manner.

Have you ever looked at a great mountain range and wondered why God made those high peaks? God could have left the mountains out of His creation. Mountains aren't really good for anything. They can't be cultivated; and beyond a certain point, they don't even grow trees. We do not need mountains in order to live on this earth.

I have flown across the trackless deserts of the West. As I looked at the endless miles of hot sand, I wondered why God made them that way. The deserts aren't good for anything. No food can grow there; the few creatures who live there are worthless to mankind.

Most impressed am I when I look at the ocean. Nobody really knows how big the ocean is. In places it is literally miles deep. It seems an awful waste. God could have fixed His creation so that rain could come without creating that vast reservoir of water. Why did He make the ocean?

God had a reason for making oceans, mountains, skies, and deserts. He never wastes anything. The psalmist said, "When I consider thy heavens. . . ." The tragedy is that many people live amid God's creation and never consider it. A thoughtless person once said to Helen Keller, "Isn't it awful to be blind?" She replied, "Not half so bad as to have two good eyes and never see anything."

I like the reply of the boy who, when someone rebuked him for saying "I seen," replied, "It is better to say 'I seen' and see something, than 'I saw' and never see anything."

We have a little dog at our house. His entire world is our backyard. He has never even noticed the sky. The only time he ever looks up into a tree is if he is trying to catch a squirrel that has climbed out of his reach. He knows us and likes to be with us, but if any strangers come into his yard, he barks at them and resents their presence. God's wonderful creation is wasted as far as our little dog is concerned.

And there are people who are content with a mighty small world. They never "consider the heavens." They never really see anything big.

When I think of the marvelous creation of the Lord—the skies and seas, mountains and deserts—and wonder why God made it all, two answers come to my mind.

## Our God Is a Great God

The psalmist says, "The heavens declare the glory of God" (Psalms 19:1). The last time I was in New York, I stood on top of the Empire State Building. I realized that whoever planned and built a building that big and high had big ideas, great abilities and resources. Little people could not have built it; they would not have even thought of it.

When you look into the face of the sky and consider something of its infinite size, you realize that no little God created it. He had to have big ideas and unlimited abilities. Truly we come to realize "Our God is a great God." Realizing His greatness, we are not so afraid of what might happen in His world. Hitlers come and go, but they cannot defeat God. Our troubles seem hard to bear, but nothing can defeat the will and purposes of the Eternal Father.

I have watched colossal storms roar across the mountains. Heavy clouds come thundering in and everything gets dark. You begin to wonder if the world isn't going to be destroyed. Then, the clouds break up and you see the green mountainside bathed in sunlight. And you know that if you wait out the storm, there will be sunlight again. When we have troubles and everything seems lost, with a picture of the greatness of God in mind, we gain courage and calmness.

On the other hand, when the sun is shining and the breezes are gentle, we know it will not always remain so. Sooner or later it will cloud up and rain again. So we make preparation during the good weather for the bad that is sure to follow. Likewise, when we are blessed with a life that is smooth and good, we remember that we must be ready for the trouble that is sure to come.

Realizing the greatness of God, our minds are stretched to take the long view of life, not living for just the moment but considering the whole. According to Greyselinck, the geologist, if a movie of the entire history of the earth were made into a film that ran for twenty-four hours, the first half of it would show history that man knows nothing about. In the twenty-four hour film, the life of man on earth would consume only the last five seconds of the film.

Such truth leads one to think in terms of eternity. A father whose son was recently killed said to me, "I could not bear it, if I thought this was the end of my boy. But God has planned far beyond this life and one accident will not wreck His plans." Such truth keeps one from surrendering to troubles, because all troubles are momentary. It makes us realize that, come sunshine or storm, life goes on toward the accomplishment of God's purposes. Nothing can defeat Him. He is greater than all His creation.

## To Think Big Thoughts

"When I consider thy heavens . . ." said the psalmist. The Bible ties man with the bigness of nature. God endowed man with the capacity to "consider" His wonderful creation. He did it for a reason. When you meditate on the bigness of skies and seas, mountains and plains, it causes you to think big thoughts. And when you begin to think big, you begin to act big.

One night soon after I had begun my own ministry, I went to preach in a little country church. I got there early and was sitting on the steps waiting for the people to come. The first one to arrive was a young man. He sat down beside me and we sat there looking at the stars and talking about how they came to be. Then I called him by name and said, "God made you, too," and we talked about his life.

At the close of my sermon that night, that young man came forward, put his hand in my hand and his life in God's hand. He felt the call to the ministry. He responded to Him who said, "Go ye into all the world and preach the gospel." He worked hard and made a good beginning, but somewhere along the way, he began to look down and lost his vision. I don't know where he is now, but I am making every effort to find him. I believe I can persuade him to look with me again into the heavens. I believe I can bring new hope to his little brokenhearted wife. And I believe God will give him another chance and that he can still make good.

It has been said:

> Two men look out through the same bars:
> One sees mud, and the other sees stars.

God put the stars there hoping we will look up and look big at life. When you see big things—like heavens, mountains, and oceans—you think big thoughts. And when you think big thoughts, your life begins to grow and you rise above a multitude of little things that would hurt you.

When Glenn Clark was a little boy, he had a nurse who foolishly tried to frighten him into being good. She told him that if little boys acted badly and didn't say their prayers, they would go blind and would not be able to see. After he went to bed and the light was turned off, he would begin to wonder if he could still see. So he would slip out of bed, go over to the window to see the stars.

"When I consider thy heavens. . . ." Some people become blind to the great things of God. Wrong living has a way of obscuring our vision. Neglect can also destroy our power to "consider the heavens." Maybe right now it would be well for you to stand before the window of prayer and look again into the face of the Father.

## God's Love and Man's Freedom

To reveal some truths about God and man and life, Jesus gave us the story of a man who planted a vineyard. The man took pains to make it complete: he put a hedge around it to protect it, dug a winepress, and even built a tower so that the workers could see any enemies who might approach. Everything possible was done to make the vineyard a good and profitable place to work.

Then the owner put the vineyard into the hands of some tenants and went to another country. At the end of the year, he sent his servants to collect the rent. Instead of paying, the tenants beat the servants and even killed one of them. The owner sent other servants, but they received the same treatment. Finally he sent his own son, feeling sure the tenants would respect him. They killed the son, thinking they could thereby possess the vineyard for themselves.

The story ends in judgment: the tenants will have to face the owner and be punished. The vineyard will be given to other tenants. Jesus concluded the story with another parable: "The stone which the builders rejected, the same is become the head of the corner" (Matthew 21:42).

In this simple story some great lessons for life are set before us, which we shall consider:

## The Providence of God

The bountiful providence of God comes first. The vineyard represents the world which God made and freely gave to man the privilege of living in. Read again the story of the creation and you will find that man was the final step in the process. God might have created man earlier and made man help Him in the work of making this world; instead, God finished the work and then made man. Isn't it wonderful how God took rivers and oceans, mountains and plains, rocks and trees, air and sky, and all the other parts and put them together in one world? Every need of man has been met.

A little boy was in the hospital. His father fixed up a large surprise-box of lovely gifts, one to be opened each day. So has God

done for us on earth. Every day man finds new surprises that God
has put here. We discover the atom with its marvelous power; it
was wonderful to open a package and find the prevention of polio;
tomorrow the package we open might be a chemical that will cure
or even prevent cancer. Isn't it even more exciting to realize there
is a God who loves people to the point where He makes such
bountiful provision for them?

A hog will eat acorns under a tree day after day, never looking
up to see where they came from. Some people are like that—but
others are led through their blessings to realize the love of their
heavenly Father.

## The Freedoms of Man

Next, consider the freedoms of man. *Freedom* is a misused and
misunderstood word. Actually, no person is free without limitations; no person is free from obligations. The owner of the
vineyard left the tenants to live as free men, yet there were some
restrictions. There was a hedge about the vineyard, and they could
use only so much land. They were not free to sleep all day; they
had responsibilities of work, and also there was rent to pay.

So is man's freedom limited. We were not free to choose the day
and generation in which we would be born, our heredity, or even
the color of our skin. Some are born with a talent to sing, others
with a talent to work with their hands. But we are all free to use our
opportunities or let them slip by, to double our talents or bury
them in the ground, to work our vineyard or let it grow up in
weeds.

I am free to be good or bad, to fill my life with hate or with love,
to live for self or to live for service, to make the world better or
worse, to count for something or to count for nothing.

Because God loves us, He desires for us our highest good. So
God doesn't just let us go and forget us; He throws around us
protecting restrictions. The Hindu poet Tagore expressed it won-
derfully: "I have on my table a violin string. It is free to move in
any direction I like. If I twist one end, it responds; it is free. But it
is not free to sing. So I take it and fix it into my violin. I bind it, and,
when it is bound, it is free for the first time to sing."

The blind Scottish preacher George Matheson wrote:

*Make me a captive, Lord,*
  *And then I shall be free;*
*Force me to render up my sword,*
  *And I shall conqueror be.*
*I sink in life's alarms*
  *When by myself I stand;*
*Imprison me within Thine arms,*
  *And strong shall be my hand.*

## Love Restricts Freedom

Because a parent loves his child and desires his highest good, he restricts the child's freedom. The child must study his lessons, eat proper food, go to bed at a reasonable hour. There are many "musts" that should be put into a child's life. Sometimes the child rebels and thinks the parent does not love him; but because love always desires to accomplish good, then love can never release the child from obligation and responsibility. Sometimes parental love degenerates into weak sentimentality which demands nothing and accomplishes nothing.

God gave to man the gift of freedom but God also gave the gift of love, and love restricts freedom. Because we love, we are not free to do some things. He gave us laws to live by; they restrict some of our freedoms but they also accomplish our higher good. God wants us to be our best, therefore He seeks to "make us His captives." The good that we develop within ourselves is the rent God wants and expects to collect from us, His tenants.

Love always desires the highest good for the one loved. A mother loves her son, so she wants him to have a healthy body. She will prepare the proper foods and patiently sit at the table coaxing him to eat. If he is sick, she will sit all night by his bedside caring for him. She wants him to be a person of fine character, so she teaches him the principles of life, works to create the right environment for him to live in, and throws around him every possible good influence.

If the child does wrong, she punishes. We smile when we say it, but it is true that punishment hurts her more than it hurts him. No matter what trouble he may get into, or how sorry he may become, his mother never gives up on him. A dear mother past eighty years had told me about the pain she was suffering; her severe arthritis gave her pain every time she moved. In the same conversation she told me of the pain in her heart because of the wrongdoings of her son. She looked at me and pitifully asked, "Why is God keeping me here?" I sat silently trying to think of an answer. But then she gave her own answer, "He is keeping me here to keep me praying for my boy."

## Love Can Be Rejected

God built a wonderful world and put His children here to live. He wants His children to be happy and wholesome, to reach their highest possibilities, to achieve their greatest good. One by one He sent men such as Elijah and Isaiah, Amos and Hosea, Jeremiah and John the Baptist, but the people rejected them.

God might have said, "I gave you clear directions how to live. You disobeyed My commands, you rejected My wisdom, you refused My love. Now you must suffer the hell of a guilty conscience, the consequences of your own stupidity, the prison of your own sins. You have had your dance—now you must pay the fiddler."

God didn't say that. Instead, "For God so loved the world, that he gave his only begotten Son, that whosoever believeth in him should not perish, but have everlasting life" (John 3:16). God did not say, "I could give My Son for your sakes, but there are no laws of justice that demand that I do so. He would have to go the length of dying on a cross, and I couldn't stand that." He didn't say that because He loves and love gives its very all.

Why do men reject God's love? We say everybody wants to be loved, but to say that is to misunderstand the meaning of true love. Jesus made the truth plain in the story of the owner of the vineyard who sent his servants and finally his own son to collect the rent from the tenants. Instead of paying the rent, the servants killed those who came.

The tenants said, ". . . come, let us kill him, and let us seize on his inheritance" (Matthew 21:38); that is, instead of accepting our responsibilities, let us serve our own selfish desires. Selfishness is the reason we reject God. We take all that He has given and use it for our own gain, our own vanity, our own comforts.

Let us never forget that the love of God has moral depth and it makes great demands. We sing silly little songs with titles such as "Somebody Up There Likes Me" and we talk about "The Man Upstairs," and we think of God's love as something that fits into a radio. But God's love demands high living. When Jesus saw men of great promise giving themselves to fish nets, He said unto them, "Follow me, and I will make you fishers of men" (Matthew 4:19). Love calls to the highest life.

To accept God's love demands that men repent of their sins and turn from their wicked ways. It caused Zaccheus to make restitution for what he had stolen; it caused Paul to come down from his lofty perch in life and give himself in service; it sent a Schweitzer into Africa. But so many men are tempted to push God out and take over for themselves. We fool ourselves when we think we can take over God's creation.

Bishop Edwin Hughes told of preaching one morning about man's stewardship. He said that everything belonged to God and that man is only a tenant here. That same day he had dinner with a farmer. That afternoon the farmer showed the preacher his fields and then said, "I have the deed to that land. Does it belong to me?" The preacher wisely said, "Ask me again a hundred years from now."

So Jesus pronounces judgment on those who reject God's love. God's judgment comes not as a result of His anger but because life simply will not work on any basis other than God's way.

My good friend Charles L. Wallis points out that some have called the disaster of crumbling buildings following the San Francisco earthquake an act of God, but a distinguished architect, after investigating the tragedy, reported, "Dishonest mortar was responsible for nearly all the earthquake damage in San Francisco." When men build their lives or their society with "dishonest mortar," eventually the judgment will come.

So Jesus said, "The stone which the builders rejected, the same is become the head of the corner . . ." (Matthew 21:42). In those days a cornerstone was used to hold two walls together. It had to be strong and sound. Sometimes the very stone needed was discarded and later the building fell. The builder might then have said, "If I had only used that stone." And those who reject Christ and His way will someday say, "If I had only followed His way, my life would not have ended in this disaster."

In Psalms 27:13, the psalmist says, "I had fainted, unless . . ." He is saying that he almost quit and would have quit except for the fact that he believed in God. He begins the psalm by saying, "The Lord is my light and my salvation; whom shall I fear?"

In the first place, faith in God always gives one faith in himself.

When people lack self-confidence, they do crazy things. Some become the dictator type. They boast and brag, swagger and strut, and seek to dominate everybody they can.

Others who feel inferior try to overcome it by retreating into a world of daydreams. Not willing to face life as it really is, they create illusions within their minds. Such a course often causes inner conflicts and can even lead to a split personality.

Then, some people are like the fox in Aesop's fable. Because he could not reach the grapes, he said they were sour and not worth reaching. One of the surest signs that a person lacks faith in himself is criticizing and belittling the accomplishments of others.

But when one puts his faith in a personal God, there comes surging into his life a wonderful strength. "The Lord is the strength of my life," the psalmist says. (*See* Psalms 27:1.) That gives a person the nerve to try.

In the second place, the psalmist had lost confidence in other people. He has a great deal to say about his enemies. He was suspicious and afraid of people. That is enough to take the heart out of anybody.

In the fourth century there lived Athanasius, a great theologian. His principles were so unpopular at the time that there arose a saying, "Athanasius against the world." He never wavered in his stand, but I dare say had one looked behind the scenes he would have found a small group of loyal friends whose love and loyalty gave him the strength that he needed.

Usually, the reason one loses faith in others is because he has developed no faith inside himself. Faith begets faith, and when the psalmist put his faith in God, faith in his fellow man naturally came, as did their faith in him.

Third, the psalmist says the thing that kept him trying was that he believed that, somehow, things would work out all right. "I had fainted," he says, "unless I had believed to see the goodness of the Lord in the land of the living" (Psalms 27:13).

## "I Almost Fainted"

In the Twenty-seventh Psalm, David tells us how he almost fainted. That is, that he almost gave up on life. Sooner or later every one of us experiences this. We are going our way, and somehow we begin to wonder if it is worth the effort. Some people do quit and bow out of life. All of us can say as the psalmist said,

"I almost fainted." However, he did not faint, and in the Twenty-seventh Psalm, he did tell how he kept from quitting and how he kept on going. Every so often, I feel that the Twenty-seventh Psalm is the one I really need.

As I read this psalm, I find myself underscoring such phrases as:

The Lord is my light and my salvation; whom shall I fear?

In the time of trouble he shall hide me.

Hear, O Lord, when I cry with my voice: have mercy also upon me and answer me.

Thou hast been my help; leave me not.

When my father and my mother forsake me, then the Lord will take me up.

I had fainted, unless I had believed to see the goodness of the Lord in the land of the living.

Wait on the Lord: be of good courage, and he shall strengthen thine heart.

In the first place, when you put your faith in God, it gives you faith in yourself. One of the greatest obstacles in the pathway to a worthwhile life is the feeling of insecurity. We all feel inadequate and overcome by the sense of inferiority. Feeling inadequate, we have a tendency to pretend superiority, then begin to bluff and bully our way through life.

On the other hand, feeling inadequate, we can retreat into a world of daydreams. Unable to face real life, we can create illusions of how we would like it to be.

The psalmist almost fainted when he looked out into a world and saw, as he put it, "False witnesses are risen up against me . . ." Time and again we reach a place when we wonder if all the world is against us.

Some time ago, in another city, I became acquainted with a man who lost both legs in an accident. People marveled at his courage and his high spirit. He told me that he almost gave up and quit, but he had a wife who loved him; whenever he was despondent and blue, she kept saying over and over to him, "Do not worry, I will always stay with you. I have two legs, and I can do the walking for you." It was her spirit that kept him going.

The psalmist not only had some friends, but when he believed in God, he believed in the future: "unless I had believed to see the goodness of the Lord in the land of the living." He believed that God would not only accomplish His will in the hereafter, but also in the here and now. The most paralyzing disaster in human nature is a persistent fear of tomorrow.

A boy born with a deformed leg had to wear a brace from the time he first began to walk. As he grew older he found he could not compete with other boys in sports. He could not run or even climb trees. Gradually he built up a feeling of inferiority. Because he felt inadequate, he developed an intense fear of life. If he could not climb a tree, how could he ever climb the ladder of life? The brace was not only on his leg; it had gotten into his mind. His father told him not to worry. Someday he would take the boy to the great cathedral, and there God would heal his leg.

Finally the day came when they were to go to the cathedral. He dressed in his best clothes. When they got to the cathedral and walked down the aisle, he could hear the brace on his leg thumping every step. He wondered if anybody around heard that thumping noise. Finally the time came for them to kneel at the altar. The father said, "Son, pray and ask God to heal you." Finally the father said, "Amen." He put his arm around the boy and said, "Son, let us give thanks to God. You are healed."

The boy said that he had never seen such a look on his father's face as he saw that day. It was a look of relief, triumph, and joy. They started down the aisle, the brace on his leg thumping just as before, but suddenly the boy said he felt the wondrously warm glow in his heart. All of a sudden he was happy. Later he explained what happened. God had not taken the brace off his leg, but He had taken the brace out of his mind. The remainder of his life he carried that brace on his leg, but he had so yielded to the marvelous power of faith that he never again feared it.

## Steps to Forgiveness

I stuck a splinter in my finger. It was not a big splinter, but I took careful pains to get it out. I knew there was the possibility of that splinter setting up an infection. And, if left alone, that infection could go up my arm and through my body, and even could kill me.

Now, the human mind is a lot like the body. The mind can be wounded. Things can get into the mind that will set up an infection that can destroy a life.

Sorrow is a wound. But sorrow is a clean wound and, unless something gets into sorrow like self-pity or bitterness, the mind wounded by sorrow will heal.

Sin is a wound. But sin is an unclean wound and, unless it is removed from the mind, it will never heal. Instead, it will go out over your nervous system and make you jumpy and jittery. It will go to your heart and accelerate its action. It will go to your stomach and upset your digestion. Sin is the wrecker of more lives than any other disease.

When I do something that violates my standards of right and wrong, I have put an unclean thing into my mind. It may not be a very big thing and, like the splinter in my finger, it may seem not to amount to much, yet even a very small wrong can set up an infection within my mind.

A prominent physician recently said to me that many of his patients did not need to see him. They needed to see a minister who could help them cleanse their conscience. Instead of sleeping pills, a lot of people need a period of old-fashioned repentance. Instead of a new drug, a lot of us need an experience of forgiveness. We need to get right with God and with our own conscience.

A person cannot do wrong and get by with it. You cannot stick a splinter in your finger and just ignore it. It must be removed. The same is true of a wrong in the mind.

Time and again, I have prescribed to people the Fifty-first Psalm. It is David's prayer of repentance. David had done wrong. He had reached the point where he could not continue to live with himself. In that prayer he prays:

"Have mercy upon me, O God." Justice is not enough. Only through God's mercy is forgiveness possible.

"I acknowledge my transgressions." He does not tell God he is no worse than somebody else. He pleads no mitigating circumstances. He frankly admits he has done wrong.

"Wash me, and I shall be whiter than snow." He has faith that forgiveness is possible. He believes that no person is hopeless in the hands of the Great Physician.

"Create in me a clean heart." He wants to be guilty no more. He is willing to change his way of living.

"Restore unto me the joy of thy salvation." He recognizes that happiness is possible only to one in a right relationship with God.

"Then will I teach transgressors thy ways." If he is healed he promises not to be ashamed of the Physician. He will tell others.

Those were the steps that David took after he had committed terrible sins, even murder. And they lead him to the place where, later, he could say, "The Lord is my shepherd; I shall not want" (Psalms 23:1). It worked for David. I have seen those very same steps work wonders in the lives of many, many people.

Some time ago Mary Pickford wrote a little book, the title of which was *Why Not Try God?* Well, why not? We have tried nearly everything else, and a lot of us are still miserable and unhappy. I said that to a person not long ago and his reply was, "I have so completely neglected God that now I am ashamed to face Him." I asked him: Would he be ashamed to face his physician if he were sick? Or would he be ashamed to face his mechanic if his car broke down? Then why be ashamed to face Him who loves us completely and who can always heal? Indeed, why not try God?

## The Man God Called a Fool

I have always felt there was something more in Jesus' story of the rich farmer than I have been able to dig out. It contains all the elements to make a great story. There is work and success, there is wealth and laughter, friends and security, wisdom and foolishness, romance and adventure, and it all ends in tragedy. But let's begin at the beginning.

It is about a man who was a farmer. Farming is probably the most ancient and satisfying profession one can follow. Adam and Eve were farmers. In their garden they grew their food and clothes, and through all the centuries we have recognized our dependence on the farmer. I know of people who claim to have no need of a pastor, or a physician, or a banker. But I have never known one to declare his independence of the farmer. If the farmers all quit work for one year, all the world would starve to death.

There is romance in farming. The farmer plows the ground and buries his seed with faith that life in the seed will burst forth, that the seasons will come and he will gather the harvest. On the farm you are close to nature. Nothing is grander than such things as the feel of new-plowed soil, the blossoms of the apple trees, the call of the bobwhite, the fragrance of new-mown hay, the clean air about you. Someone has said that the typical American success story is the boy who grows up on a farm, moves to the city, works hard and makes money, buys a farm and moves back to live on it.

This man was rich. His ground "brought forth plentifully." So much so that he had no place to store all he produced. I have heard of people who had so much money they did not know what to do with it. I don't know any people like that. I wish I did. I would cultivate their friendship and do my best to help them solve that particular problem.

I know of a preacher who once preached a sermon called "What I Would Do With A Million Dollars." After the service a man came up and handed him a check for that amount. I wish that same man would come to hear me preach. I am not mad at rich people; I like to have them around.

This farmer was interested in saving what he made. That is not wrong. God saves. When God created the earth, He put a lot of water on it and through all the centuries He has kept every drop of it. Not one grain of the earth's sand has ever been lost. After Jesus fed the multitude, He had the disciples gather up the fragments that none be wasted.

To be a successful farmer requires hard work, so we know this man was not lazy. There is no hint of dishonesty in the story. We must assume that he paid his workers a fair wage, that he sold his goods at the right price. He was not excessively greedy. He did not try to buy up all the land in the country. In fact, when he found he had enough for his needs, he was willing to stand back and let others have an opportunity. Still, God called him a fool.

## Why He Was a Fool

For the answer turn back to Psalm 14:1. There we read, "The fool hath said in his heart, There is no God." If you asked that rich farmer, "Do you believe there is a God?" doubtless he would have said, "Certainly I do." He could have given many reasons why he so believed, but all of his reasons would have been from his mind.

When it came to his feelings, his heart, he had left God out. Why? Because he did not feel the need of God. There is a vast difference between believing in your mind and believing in your heart. I have had people talk to me about divine healing and say they believed there is something to it. On the other hand, in the middle of the night I have gone to the hospital to pray with a father and mother whose baby was about to die. Their belief is vastly different because they feel the need so deeply.

We can talk about the forgiveness of sin and say we believe in it. But let some person sit in the pastor's study or kneel at the altar whose soul is darkened by a deep sense of guilt. He might have tried forgetting it, thinking of something else, moral reform, but nothing has worked. The peace and laughter have gone out of his life, and in their place dwell remorse and fear. As that person looks up to God, it is not mere intellectual belief; it comes from the heart.

The possession of wealth is not wrong. Jesus never said it was. But it is the most dangerous thing in life. Jesus talked about money more than any other subject. Remember this: He was talking to poor people. Many times we hear people say, "I don't want to be rich. All I want is just enough to live on comfortably and to take care of me when I get old." That is all the farmer in Jesus' story wanted, but God called him a fool.

Jesus said at the conclusion of this story, "So is he that layeth up treasure for himself, and is not rich toward God." This man thought about himself. He talks about "My fruits," "My goods," "My barns." He says, "I shall do this," "I shall do that." My— My—My—I—I—I.

Instead of gratitude, his success brought pride. Instead of a sense of obligation to his fellow man, he thought only of his own pleasure and needs. Instead of faith in God, he put his confidence in things.

The man reached the point that he felt no need of God. He was sufficient unto himself. Jesus said such a person is a fool. It worries me to hear someone say, "It is my duty to go to church." I don't want anybody coming to my church out of a sense of duty. I want people to come from a sense of need. It is not necessary to talk to a thirsty man about the body's need of water. You only have to put the water before him.

When a person thinks about things, measures success by his possessions, is mainly interested in his body, his physical needs and desires, he forgets his soul and he ceases to hunger and thirst for God. He may still think there is a God, but if in his heart he does not feel it, then that person is a fool.

## Treasure Where We Are Going

The favorite story of Sigmund Freud, the father of psychiatry, was about a sailor who was shipwrecked on one of the South Sea Islands. The natives lifted him to their shoulders and marched triumphantly into their village. The sailor doubtless thought he was to be their main dish for dinner that night. But to his astonishment, they put him on a throne, put a crown on his head, and proclaimed him as their king.

He was the absolute ruler. Every native was his servant. He enjoyed his new station in life, but after a while he began to wonder about it all. He discretely asked some questions, and he found that it was their custom once each year to make some man a king, king for a year. He also learned that at the end of his year, the king was banished to an island where he starved to death.

The sailor did not like that, but being a resourceful fellow, he put his mind to work and he hit upon a marvelous solution. Because he was king, his orders were obeyed. So he put the natives to building boats. When they had enough boats, he started transplanting fruit trees to the island where he was to be sent. He had the carpenters go there and build comfortable houses, the farmers he set to clearing up the land and planting crops. So, when his kingship was over he had a place of abundance to which to go.

We readily admit the wisdom of that man. The kings before him acted very foolishly in not looking ahead to the time they would no longer be king. Of course, one can become so absorbed in his present possessions and pleasures that he has no time nor inclination to look ahead.

There was the rich farmer that Jesus told us about. He became so blinded by his success and sense of well-being that he could not look ahead to his future needs. "But God said unto him, Thou fool, this night thy soul shall be required of thee: then whose shall those things be, which thou hast provided?" (Luke 12:20). He forgot that one day his kingship would end and that he would have to leave all those things behind him.

God has given to each of us the kingship over our own lives. We can become so intoxicated with the things we have that we forget that before us, somebody else possessed those things and after we are gone there will be another king. Actually, we are kings for only a little while, then we move on to another life. Jesus tried to warn us. He said, "In my Father's house are many mansions" (John

14:2). He said, "Lay up for yourselves treasures in heaven" (Matthew 6:20).

We say success is determined by the wealth we accumulate. It depends on the wealth in which place: that which we will have for a few short years, or that which we shall have forever? The wealth that counts is accumulated by a soul that has learned to pray, by a conscience that is clear, by a life that is dedicated, by a fellowship with Him who owns the land on both sides of the river. This was the wealth that one man swapped for barns. God did not say he was bad. He said he was a fool.

## Commitment Brings Courage

The Prophet Isaiah said, "And thine ears shall hear a word behind thee, saying, This is the way, walk ye in it . . ." (Isaiah 30:21). We are not compelled to walk alone through life. Neither must we remain dependent upon our own wisdom. We may abide in the supporting presence of the eternal God and His guidance.

The first and greatest decision toward making life worthwhile is commitment to God's way and God's will. If you say, "I have never heard the voice of God behind me," you may need to remember that God does not waste His breath. He speaks only to people who are ready and willing to listen. Hearing the voice of God, you need to begin walking.

You concentrate on your problems, and you get confused. Make up your mind you are going to walk God's way, no matter what happens. You make one decision, and the other decisions of life just fall into place. You begin getting somewhere.

In the second place, a consciousness that you are walking in God's way enables you to face the future with anticipation, instead of apprehension. Most of the confusion and disturbance in our minds results from fear of what might happen in the future. Someone has said that forty percent of our fears are things that might happen in the future; twelve percent are of some imaginary illness; ten percent are fears for loved ones; thirty percent are over something that happened in the past, about which nothing that can now be done. Only eight percent of our fears have real causes.

The way to rid your mind of fear is through the substitution of stronger thoughts. When you feel the voice of God in your heart, fears disappear, and you move triumphantly through life. Many years ago, Ernest Holmes was in a hotel room in San Francisco, when his phone rang, and a voice said, "I am in room 606 and I am in trouble." Mr. Holmes discovered the man was drinking, but he was quite rational. He went to see him. On the table was a bottle half-filled with whiskey. He listened to the man's story, in which he said that he lacked the power to break the hold that alcohol had upon him.

Ernest Holmes said, "You stay here. I am going to my room to pray. I will leave the bottle beside you, but you will never finish it." In his room Holmes began to picture in his mind that man having the power to resist his craving. He thought about the strength he could possess by the grace of God. He formed his prayer to fit the picture of this man. As he prayed he concentrated upon the man's strength instead of his weakness. Holmes reported that early the next morning his phone rang. "Come here quickly," the man said. When Holmes got there, he saw that none of the liquor was gone from the bottle. The man was pacing the floor. He said, "Last night I felt that God was in this room. I conquered my desire. I am now set free."

There are two comments upon that story that I wish to make: When one takes God into his life he begins to concentrate on his powers instead of problems; when one finds fellowship with God, he has strengths that overcome every weakness. You cannot be the same person after you become God's person. Commitment of life gives a courageous heart.

## Sustained and Strengthened

In his play *Candle in the Wind*, Maxwell Anderson tells the story of a young American girl pitted against the ruthless Nazi rulers of occupied Paris. She was only a young girl, as he put it, just a "candle in the wind." But the feeling that she was an American citizen sustained and strengthened her. She felt that behind her was the might and power of her beloved nation and that her cause was one of justice and right.

Sometimes we feel no stronger than a "candle in the wind." But when we experience the assurance of God's power and presence, we become sustained and strengthened.

Whittier said it beautifully in "The Eternal Goodness":

> *Yet, in the maddening maze of things,*
> *And tossed by storm and flood,*

*To one fixed trust my spirit clings;*
*I know that God is good.*

## Strength That Makes Living Fun

Henry van Dyke wrote these marvelous words:

*This is the gospel of labour, ring it, ye bells of the kirk!*
*The Lord of Love came down from above, to live with men who work.*

Many people feel overburdened; their day's work seems just too much. However many people have learned that there are resources available equal to the very hardest work and biggest job. The Bible gives us a marvelous promise: "But they that wait upon the Lord shall renew their strength; they shall mount up with wings as eagles; they shall run, and not be weary; and they shall walk, and not faint" (Isaiah 40:31).

Someone asked Thomas Edison why he worked so hard. He replied, "I have not worked a day in my life; I have just had a good time."

We can rise above those things that hurt—the disappointments, defeat, and wearisome hours—and we can find the strength that makes living so much fun.

# 2

## *The Second Spiritual Wonder:*

# The Miracle of Salvation Through Jesus Christ

 Let's begin with the question "Who is Jesus?" That is a thrilling, yet difficult question. In seeking an answer to that question, I could very easily turn to my books and read what many others have said about Him. But as I faced that question, I felt impressed just to sit for a time and think about Him. One by one, the pictures of Him in my mind began coming into view. I saw a lovely young mother sitting in a stable by a manger. I heard a baby cry. I saw a young man living in a tiny village. I saw this young man growing up and taking on family responsibilities. He was about thirty years of age when He went out and began to preach. For three years He walked about the countryside and talked to the people who would listen. He must have been a lonely man, though He made friends and at times was surrounded by multitudes. Still, in every man there is a deep longing for a home, for a woman he loves, for little children to call his own. Jesus never had that. Just my own fellowship with Him makes me know He is more than Jesus. I know He is Jesus Christ.

I know of no person who really questions the fact that a man named Jesus once lived in Galilee. We are familiar with the existing records of His life and the kind of a man He was. And, as we come to know about His earthly life, we can say with the poet Richard Gilder:

> *If Jesus Christ is a man*
> *And only a man—I say*

> *That of all mankind I cleave to him,*
> *And to him will cleave alway.*

But as we come to know about Jesus even from the cold printed words of the four Gospels, we begin to feel a closeness to Him and love for Him, and He begins to have a strange power over us. We become sure—really sure—that He was more than just a man. And so, we can say again with Richard Gilder:

> *If Jesus Christ is a God—*
> *And only a God,—I swear*
> *I will follow him through heaven and hell,*
> *The earth, the sea, the air.*

The strongest proof that Jesus is the Christ is not what He once did on earth, but what He does today. I profoundly believe in the miracles of Christ. I studied each one of them carefully, and I wrote a book entitled *The Touch of the Master's Hand,* which is still selling in the bookstores throughout the land. But, the great significance of the miracles is the fact that He still does them. There was a man who had sold the furniture in his little home to buy liquor, but then he became a Christian. One day a friend sneeringly said to him, "You don't really believe that yarn about Jesus turning the water into wine?" The man replied, "I'm an ignorant man. I don't know about water and wine. But I know this, that Jesus Christ turned liquor into furniture in my house. And that is a good enough miracle for me."

A number of times I have sailed in a little boat on the Sea of Galilee, and, of course, I would think about Jesus stilling the storm on that sea. When I was there, there was no storm and I saw no miracle. But through more than forty years as the pastor of a church, I have seen many, many people in whose hearts our Lord stilled the storm after some great sorrow, hurt, or disappointment. I know He is still working His miracles.

Many years ago, I offered through a newspaper column I wrote a small billfold-size picture of Christ. I was not prepared for the requests that I received, and eventually sent out more than 100,000 copies of that little picture. I received hundreds of letters as a result of those pictures. One man wrote me that he lost his billfold with a considerable sum of money in it. A few days later he received it in the mail with a note from the finder saying, "When I first found this I fully intended to keep the money. But when I looked at that picture of Christ, I had to send it back." Even a *picture* of Him does something to people. Of course, He was more than just a man.

There are four facts about Christ which I firmly believe:

1. Christ was born without an earthly father. His birth was different from that of any other person who has ever lived. He was not an actual man; He was supernatural. God sent an angel to a pure young woman who told her that she would give birth to the Son of the Highest. She was puzzled, and answered, "How shall this be, seeing I know not a man?" The angel told her that the Holy Ghost would be His Father (*see* Luke 1:26–35). He was God even before He was born.

2. When He lived on earth He had supernatural power. The winds and the waves obeyed His voice. He could heal sickness; He could even raise the dead. He could take one little boy's lunch and feed a multitude of five thousand. He could forgive sin; He could put a song into a broken heart; He could bring hope to the discouraged and strength to the weary. With Nicodemus I say, "No man can do these miracles that thou doest, except God be with him" (John 3:2). He imparted power to others and it is still available to people today.

3. I believe that His death on the cross is my doorway to eternal life. His cross is an example of sacrifice, and it is a revelation of God's love—but it is more—much more. That Friday, He did something that forever makes a difference in my relationship with God. For these first disciples it was "black Friday." Their Leader was crucified. It seemed that God had forsaken His Own. But later on those disciples realized, as Saint Paul put it, "God was in Christ, reconciling the world unto himself . . ." (2 Corinthians 5:19). And when people realized that, then they saw the cross—not as God's desertion of man—but as God's saving power. Then black Friday became Good Friday.

4. I believe that Christ rose from the dead, and His Resurrection is my assurance that there is life for me beyond the grave. "Because I live," He said, "ye shall live also" (John 14:19). I love the life we have here, but I know in a little while someone will carry my body and bury it in the ground. There it will decay, but because I know Christ, I know that will not be the end of me. I shall live after death.

Jesus Christ is the most loved Person that ever lived on this earth. I often ask myself why, and really, I think it's because He is our best Friend.

An English publication offered the prize for the best definition of a friend. Many answers were received and the one that was given first prize was this: "A friend is one who comes in when the whole world goes out." That is a mighty good definition.

Young Joseph Scriven was deeply in love with a girl. They planned to marry, but she was accidentally drowned. For months he was bitter and heartbroken. Later he had a deep experience of Christ in his heart, and he wrote these very familiar lines:

*What a friend we have in Jesus,*
*All our sins and griefs to bear!*

I think there is, however, a better definition of a friend. Once Henry Ford was having lunch with a man, when suddenly he asked the man, "Who is your best friend?" The man was not sure, and then Ford said, "I will tell you who your best friend is." He took out a pencil and wrote on the tablecloth this sentence: "Your best friend is he who brings out the best that is within you."

Jesus had a way of making people believe two things about themselves. First, I ought not to be the way I am. Second, I need not stay the way I am.

In every one of us there is a mixture of the best and the worst. Every human heart is an unseen battlefield where the good and the bad are fighting it out. Sometimes the one wins and sometimes the other wins. When the bad wins out, we are ashamed and disgusted with ourselves. But when the good wins, we have a clean feeling inside and we are filled with joy. Jesus brings out our best and that is why we love Him so.

One of my best friends in the ministry is Dr. Asbury Lenox. Recently, he told me this story: A man of a different theology came into his study to talk with him. They talked, but they did not find many points of agreement. The man got up to go, and as he was walking out the door, he turned and said to Dr. Lenox, "Preacher, we can get together on Jesus."

I know that Christian people have different opinions about things, but somehow, I also know that "we can get together on Jesus."

## Meet the Master

He was born of poor parents in a village in an insignificant little country. When He was twelve years old, He was conscious of the fact that God had placed Him here for a specific purpose. At the age of thirty, He made public His plans and purposes and began the three short years of His public ministry.

He loved people and enjoyed being with them. He went to their parties; He was a popular dinner guest; even the little children crowded around Him. He invited twelve men to work with Him, and later He commissioned them to carry on His work. He told a ruler about an experience called the "new birth."

He offered an outcast woman water that would quench the thirst of her very soul. He healed the sick, raised the dead, opened the eyes of the blind, loosed the tongues of the dumb, brought hearing to the deaf, and caused the lame to walk. He fed those who were hungry, and brought peace to troubled minds.

He taught the people that happiness comes from the inside, that the solution to hates and prejudices is not in laws but in love. He told of the amazing power of prayer, that the treasures one lays up in heaven are more important than the treasures one accumulates on earth, that a divided heart leads to destruction.

Faith in God was to Him a matter of supreme importance. Because God so beautifully clothed the lilies of the field, and because God cared so tenderly for even the birds of the air, He concluded that humans who are to live eternally should not worry about the things of this life. Instead, one should seek God's Kingdom first and the other things of life would be taken care of.

He warned against people judging each other. He warned that a life built on any other principles than the ones He taught would be like a house built on sand that would not stand in the face of a storm.

He said that His Kingdom was like the growth of the tiny seed that eventually becomes a tree, or like the leaven that eventually leavens the entire loaf. And that possessing Him was worth all else one had, just as the merchant sold all his possessions in order to own the one pearl of supreme worth.

When one of His disciples suggested, after a marvelous worship experience, that He just continue there, He refused. Every mountaintop experience of worship was translated by Him into acts of service and of living. He said that the way to become great was to become a servant.

Firmly He taught that one is never justified in holding an unforgiving spirit. To a crowd which was preparing to stone a sinner to death, He suggested that the one without sin cast the first stone. And to the sinner He said, "Neither do I condemn thee, go and sin no more." He loved sinners and freely forgave everyone who would accept forgiveness.

Simple stories from everyday life illustrated the eternal principles He taught: the Samaritan who turned aside to help one in need, the foolish rich man who thought of his physical needs but forgot his soul, the shepherd who hunted until he found just one lost sheep, the father who welcomed his prodigal son home, and many, many more.

He wept with friends who had lost a loved one by death. He was disappointed when some people He had healed expressed no gratitude. He pointed out that God expects every person to do his part, even though he may have only one talent.

He cursed a fig tree for not producing fruit. He drove people out of the church who were misusing it. He said that we have duties to our government and duties to God. He praised a widow who gave a small gift.

He did not want to die, but He chose death rather than lower His standards. But as He died He prayed for the forgiveness of those who were killing Him, He gave comfort to a man dying with Him, He thought of the care of His mother, and He expressed His faith in God.

Three days after He was buried, He came back to life. He spoke to a woman, He encouraged some disheartened people, He spoke peace to His disciples, and one morning He even cooked their breakfast. He told His few followers to carry on His work until it covers the world, and finally He ascended into heaven.

He is today the one hope of the world. He is Jesus Christ, the Son of God and the Saviour of man.

## Kneel at the Cross

In Bunyan's *Pilgrim's Progress*, Pilgrim was making his way from the City of Destruction to the City Celestial, with a heavy burden on his back. Finally he came to a hill called Calvary. He climbed the

hill and humbly knelt at the foot of the Cross. As he knelt, his
burden rolled away and was buried in a sepulcher.

Millions of others can testify to that same experience. Many
people really know the meaning of that little chorus:

> At the cross, at the cross, where I first saw the light,
> And the burden of my heart rolled away.
> It was there by faith I received my sight,
> And now I am happy all the day.

I want to say something about the Cross, yet words are so
inadequate. I feel like a little boy trying to dip the ocean dry with
his tiny bucket. The Cross means so much, its meaning is so
profound that, instead of trying to explain it, we just kneel before
it with deepest reverence and humility.

First, the Cross is a revelation of God's love for all men.
Dr. Maltby, in his book *The Meaning of the Cross*, tells of a boy who
did many mean and terrible things. His father finally said, "I
washed my hands of him."

Whatever might be the complete opposite of washing your
hands of someone, God did it on the Cross. We may do cowardly
and disappointing things and bring deep pain to the Father's heart,
but in the Cross we see that He never gives us up. Even when the
love of Jesus was thrown in His face with spitting and mocking and
cursing, it remained unbroken. He was pierced but went on
loving.

On a dark night, a man stood by himself on the deck of a ship.
Suddenly he heard a roaring and then a nearby volcano burst into
flame. The whole country round about was lighted; then the flame
died. For a short time, he said, was revealed the fire that is ever
burning in the heart of the mountain.

As we see the Cross, we see the love that is forever in the heart
of God for each of us. But the Cross did more than reveal God's
love. Something happened that day on Calvary that forever makes
a difference in the relationship between man and God. Something
once and for all was done that day.

As a boy of twelve, Jesus said, "Wist ye not that I must be about
my Father's business?" (Luke 2:49). He came for a specific purpose
and on the Cross He said, "It is finished" (John 19:30). Every task
was completed, God's will was accomplished, prophecy was
fulfilled, man's redemption was secured.

As someone has said: "There was no other good enough to pay the price of sin; He only could unlock the gates of heaven and let us in." His death on the Cross was not just another martyr's death. It was different from anything that has ever happened in the history of the world. It was something done once and for all. It had never been done before and will never be done again.

About the year 1830, a man named George Wilson killed a government employee who caught him in the act of robbing the mails. He was tried and sentenced to be hanged. However, the President of the United States, Andrew Jackson, sent him a pardon. But Wilson did a strange thing. He refused to accept the pardon and no one seemed to know what to do. So the case was carried to the Supreme Court of the United States. Chief Justice John Marshall, perhaps the greatest chief justice we have ever had, wrote the opinion. In it he said, "A pardon is a slip of paper, the value of which is determined by the acceptance of the person to be pardoned. If it is refused, it is no pardon. George Wilson must be hanged." And he was.

The death of Christ on the Cross is the pardon God has sent. Before it becomes a pardon for me I must accept it in faith and obedience. It is through the Cross, and only that way, that one can be saved.

His was not the only cross on Calvary that day. Two other men died with Him. One sneered at Him. But the other said with humble faith, "Lord, remember me." He was a man who had done mean and shoddy things, but because of his faith Jesus said to him, "Today shalt thou be with me in paradise" (Luke 23:43).

Fanny Crosby, who wrote many wonderful hymns, such as "Blessed Assurance," "Rescue the Perishing," "Face to Face," and "Close to Thee," was herself won to Christ through a hymn. In church one day the people were singing:

> *Alas, and did my Saviour bleed?*
> *And did my Sov'reign die?*
> *Would He devote the sacred head*
> *For such a worm as I?*

Fanny recorded in her biography, "During the singing my very soul was flooded with celestial light." No person can explain such an experience. It goes past human understanding, but many know that such experiences do come to those who believe.

## Jesus' Seven Words on the Cross

It is a stimulating and helpful experience to put before oneself the seven sentences of Christ on the Cross. So I am listing them in the order it is generally believed they were spoken by our Lord.

1. "Father, forgive them; for they know not what they do" (Luke 23:34). Jesus had very real grievances—the rulers had opposed Him and plotted His death, His disciples had betrayed Him, the people had chosen sorry Barabbas over Him, His trial had been unjust, He had been mocked, cursed and spit upon, and all His friends had deserted Him. But when He prays for the forgiveness of "them" He means all of them. There is no bitterness in His heart. In a beautiful act of charity, He even excuses them and seeks to remove their guilt by saying they do not know what they do. This is surely a time for each of us to throw the blanket of love and forgiveness over those who have done us wrong—to wipe the slate clean by extending our own forgiveness to those who have wronged us.

2. "Today shalt thou be with me in paradise" (Luke 23:43). It was the word of hope for a wasted and misspent life. It reveals the heart of the Eternal that is ever eager to reclaim and restore even the least and the last of the lost. It is His word that this life is not the end but rather the entrance into a larger one.

3. "Woman, behold thy son. . . . Behold thy mother" (John 19:26, 27). Even as He is suffering the agony of death, He has a word of compassion and concern for one whom He loves. In the midst of more pain than it seems anyone could bear, He still is anxious about the needs and well-being of another. Here is a rebuke to selfishness, a shame for hardheartedness. It reveals that we ourselves are living at our very best when we can turn away from our own sorrows and disappointments and seek to meet a need in a weaker life.

4. "My God, my God, why hast thou forsaken me?" (Mark 15:34). This is the only question He ever asked God, and I believe it to be a very real one. It is His human side that is so clearly revealed here in a momentary sense of forsakenness—an experience that we all have some time or another. Every person somewhere along the way of life feels that God has let him down. It is good to recall in such times that the Resurrection followed the Crucifixion. Victory is always the last word with God.

5. "I thirst" (John 19:28). Here is represented the physical price that Christ paid—the cost of something grand and glorious. There are no shortcuts to the things that really matter. And, also, it represents His very deep thirst for God at that moment. In the midst of suffering, even He who was so close is drawn even closer to the Father. Not always is that so. A sorrow makes us either bitter or better. But for those who will see and feel, God is closer in times of deep sorrow than at any other time.

6. "It is finished" (John 19:30). I think the soldiers who were at the front when the Armistice came can understand better than any of us all that is wrapped up in those words of our Lord. The blood of the battlefield, the agony of the strain of battle, the homesickness in a faraway land, and then—"It is finished"—the victory is won. That is what Christ felt, only on a much grander scale. His task was finished. His Kingdom was planted, and the "gates of hell shall not prevail against it." (*See* Matthew 16:18.)

7. "Father, into thy hands I commend my spirit" (Luke 23:46). It was a cry of faith. He had done His best. He had given His all. Now He was willing to leave the results to God. And we, too, when we have done our best, need not worry or fear. God always takes care of the results. This was also a cry of refuge—even as we sing:

> *Jesus, Lover of my soul,*
> *Let me to Thy bosom fly. . . .*
> *Safe into the haven guide;*
> *O receive my soul at last.*

What great words to have before us throughout life—the seven sentences of Christ on the Cross!

## The Forgiving Father

The most divinely tender and humanly touching story ever told on earth is the story Jesus told us of the father welcoming home his wayward boy. We call it the story of "The Prodigal Son." But really it should be called the story of "The Forgiving Father." Jesus told it to reveal God's attitude to us when we have done wrong (Luke 15:11–24). In this story Jesus leads up to the grand climax of the father's love by the staircase of the boy's life:

1. The first step is self-will. "Give me. . . . The younger son gathered all together and took his journey into a far country." Home was irksome. The young man wanted freedom. He was tired of the rules and restraints of the father. He wanted to live his life as he pleased. The father made no attempt to hold him. Had the father held the boy against his will, home would have become a prison and the father a jailer.

The Pharisees set up an elaborate system of laws and regulations and attempted to force people to accept them. Not so with the religion of Christ. He shows us the way, but it is entirely a voluntary matter whether or not one follows that way. If we wish we can choose some other way with perfect freedom.

2. The second step is this: "He began to be in want." His once radiant spirit becomes as bedraggled as his clothes. One can live away from God and never want for material things. We see that demonstrated again and again. But there is a deeper and more real want. It is the longing of one's heart, the thirst of one's soul in the far country away from God.

In an effort to satisfy his wants, "he went and joined himself to a citizen of that country; and he sent him into the fields to feed swine." Note carefully that word *sent*. Now where is his boasted freedom? He who lives to do as he likes eventually becomes the slave of his likes. Someone has well said, "No one ever breaks the laws of God. He breaks himself instead of the laws."

3. "And when he came to himself" is the third step. No man is a single self. There is our passionate self, which, when it gives way to such passions as fear, lust, or hate, controls our thinking and actions, and brings us down to the level of beasts. There is our greedy self, which gives no thought to the rights and feelings of others. And there is our careless self, which just drifts along without bothering to think.

And then there is our best self, the self that Shakespeare meant when he said, "To thine own self be true." We sometimes say, "I was not myself," which is an accurate expression. When, in the far country, he looked into the face of a hog and realized the level to which he had sunk, that prodigal boy knew he was not himself.

4. Not from outer compulsion but from an inner awakening, he now takes the fourth step: "Father I have sinned. . . . Make me. . . ." There is the key that unlocks the door of home. Without it no one can ever re-enter. There is no pardoning mercy even from

the Father of mercy until we repent. There is no forgiveness possible for one who feels no need of repentance.

One definition of repentance is to change one's mind in regard to one's conduct. The experience of repentance comes when one becomes convinced that his way has been the wrong way, when he is genuinely sorry for his sin, sorry to the point where he is willing to keep forever from his evil way, no matter what the cost.

And so the boy said, "Make me as one of thy hired servants." He realized he was not quite as big as he thought he was. Before, he had said, "Give me . . ." but later he realized that it was not what he could get from his father that was important, but what his father could do for him and through him that counted. So with God. God pours His blessings freely on the just and the unjust. But when we let Him, God will work in us and through us a high purpose in life.

5. Now comes the main step. "When he was yet a great way off, his father saw him, and had compassion, and ran, and fell on his neck, and kissed him," and restored him. No period of waiting, no sharp reproof. The forgiveness is complete.

The loving forgiveness of God is what makes life bearable. In the lives of most of us there is a shameful chapter. We can take the way of Judas Iscariot or the way of Simon Peter. Both sinned, and neither could bear his sin. Judas went out and hanged himself, but Peter came back to Christ. The old song is ever new and ever needed.

> He breaks the power of canceled sin,
> He sets the prisoner free;
> His blood can make the foulest clean;
> His blood availed for me.

# 3

## *The Third Spiritual Wonder:*

# The Assurance of Eternal Life

 One of the most thrilling experiences of my ministry was preaching in a service on the Isle of Patmos. I stood on a large rock just above the cave in which John wrote the Book of Revelation. Sitting out before me were about four hundred people. It was my privilege to give the sermon.

I turned to the twenty-first chapter of the Book of Revelation and I began reading: "And I saw a new heaven and a new earth: for the first heaven and the first earth were passed away; and there was no more sea." The last phrase took hold of me: ". . . and there was no more sea." From that spot I could look in every direction at the sea which surrounded that little island. Suddenly, I realized what John felt. The sea was his prison—the sea kept him from going where he wanted to go and doing what he wanted to do. The sea was his handicap. As he looked into the City of God, he realized the prison doors would be opened; the handicaps would be taken away; there he would have the ability and the opportunity to realize all of his hopes—to accomplish all of his dreams.

I thought of Fanny J. Crosby. From the time she was a tiny baby she was blind. She wrote many wonderful hymns, but many of us feel that maybe her best hymn was written out of this very experience. She wrote:

> *Some day the silver cord will break,*
> *And I no more as now shall sing;*

*But O, the joy when I shall wake*
*Within the palace of the King!*
*And I shall see Him face to face. . . .*

That was her idea of heaven—the ability to see.

I remember once after a service, when I had been preaching on eternal life, a man who had no arms came up and spoke to me. Both of his arms had been cut off in an accident. He asked, "When I get to heaven, will I have some arms?" That's what it meant to him.

I think of our dear black friends in the days of slavery. They would cook the dinner and wait on the table and stand back for other people to eat. I can understand something of how they felt. When I was a little boy going around with my father to his churches, on Sundays people would invite us home to dinner. They would always have more people than could eat at the first table, so the children would have to wait. It seemed so long and when we finally did get to eat, there was nothing left of the chicken but the wings and the backs and pieces nobody else wanted. So I can understand those dear people in the long ago who had to wait. As they dreamed of the City of God, they sang, "I'm going to eat at the welcome table one of these days."

I once preached at a school in Talladega, Alabama. At that time it was the largest school in the world for blind and deaf children. I preached there for several days in a large auditorium filled with children from kindergarten through high school. All of the children on one side of the building were blind; they could not see me. Those on the other side were deaf, and a teacher interpreted with her hands as I spoke.

On the grounds was a little cottage. The first morning I was there, I went over to this cottage. Inside there were five children who could neither hear, nor see, nor speak. As I went in, there was a little boy sitting just inside the door on the floor. They told me he was five years old, but he was little and frail for his age. I picked him up and he put his little arms around my neck. The entire time I was there, he held on just as tightly as he could. Finally, it was time for me to go and I had to take his little hands and pull them away and sit him down. He cried. It was the most pitiful crying I ever heard. The remaining days that I was there, I would go over to that cottage and get that little boy every morning after breakfast.

I would pick him up and he would put his arms around my neck. I would walk with him for a time around the campus.

Gradually, he put his arms around my heart, and I began to feel some bitterness and resentment toward God. I found myself saying, "God, You are not fair. You are not just. You are not loving. This little boy has done nothing wrong. He does not deserve this, but You let him be born so that he could not hear, nor see, nor speak."

Then it seemed the Lord patted me on the shoulder and said, "Now, Charles, just settle down. This is not the entire story. There will come a day when I will open his little eyes, unstop his ears, and loose his tongue."

What is your dream? What is your bitterest disappointment? Tell me what it is and I can tell you what heaven means to you.

One of the most moving experiences I ever had was during a Thanksgiving service at Grace Church in Atlanta while I was pastor there. The church was filled with people and we were singing:

> *Come, ye thankful people, come—*
> *Raise the song of harvest home.*

As we sang, I happened to notice a couple sitting on the second seat. They had had one son; he was a wonderful boy. He had graduated from Georgia Tech and was going into the army for two years. The night before he was to leave, the three of them attended church together. I saw them kneel at the altar with this boy between his mother and father. I did not hear the prayers of that father and mother, but I know what those prayers were. They were praying, "God watch over our boy and bring him back home safely." He went to Korea and he had only been there for a few months when the message came that their son had been killed in action. It was these parents who were singing, "Come, ye thankful people, come."

I looked a little farther back and I saw a lady I had known for some years, her hair now streaked with gray. I knew that her greatest desire was to be married and have a home and have children. At the time when she could have married, both her father and mother were invalids. There was nothing else for her to do but stay at home and care for them. Her father died eight years later; her mother died twelve years later. Now her chance was gone. She lived in an apartment alone. But she was singing, "Come, ye thankful people, come."

I saw this one and I saw that one, but away back in the corner was a man I especially noticed. He was a man about thirty-five years old. His record was such that he would get in jail and get out—then get in again and get out. Every time he got out of jail he would come to my office to see me. He would usually get there just before lunchtime. There was a little restaurant down the street and I would say to him, "Let's go down and eat lunch and we can talk there." He was always ready to go, and we became real good friends. Gradually, he told me his story. As a little boy he lived on one of the sorriest, poorest streets in Atlanta. He did not remember his mother. He and his father lived alone together. He told me how they didn't have any cooking utensils. His father would open a can of beans or something and heat it on a gas jet and they would eat out of the can. The only place he had to play was that dirty street. Nobody ever kissed him goodnight, or tucked him into bed. Nobody ever taught him to say his prayers before he went to bed. That was the chance that he had. But—there he was that day singing, "Come, ye thankful people, come."

As I saw so many people, suddenly I said to myself, "Thank God for the Judgment Day!" Until that moment I had always been afraid of the Judgment Day. I dreaded the time when God would open the book to the page on which my name was written and read all the things I had done wrong and judge me. But that day I realized that isn't what it's all about. There is going to come a day when the wrongs of life will be righted.

## The Place Named Heaven

"I go to prepare a place for you," said Jesus (John 14:2). Underscore that word *place*. Before God made people, He made a place for them to live. He anticipated all the needs of mankind and He took care of those needs in the creation of this world.

God knew that man's body would require food, so He created soil in which things could grow. Man appreciates beauty, so there are majestic mountains, colorful birds, precious stones, lovely flowers, blue skies, and so much else. Man needs to satisfy his spirit of adventure, so God made a big world in which man could roam and explore.

In the world God hid many things for man to search out. It took thousands of years before the source of electricity was discovered. Man discovered how to send sound through the air, and then pictures, and now we have radio and television. It seems like just the other day we learned how to release the power within the atom.

To live on earth, man needs lots of water. His fields must be watered or nothing will grow. He needs water to drink and to bathe in. God worked out for man the finest water system that can be imagined: the oceans are the giant reservoirs; the sun draws the water up into the clouds, and the winds blow the clouds over the earth, and the rain falls; the water serves its purposes and then returns to the ocean. In the process it is purified and the same water can be used over and over again.

What a wonderful world God has prepared for us! Yet it contains many challenges for man, and in meeting these challenges man develops himself. I do not know why God included in the world the illnesses of yellow fever, polio, cancer, and so many other diseases. But little by little man is learning to overcome these enemies of his body. Someday man will even learn how to cope with cyclones and hurricanes.

## A Place to Grow

What kind of place is heaven? Judging from the kind of place God made for us here, and judging from what we know about Christ, we can pretty well know some things about heaven.

Jesus said, "I go to prepare a place for you." Surely heaven is a place where we can continue to grow and develop. Jesus was a Teacher here on earth; surely He is the same in the Father's house. The Bible says, "Now we see through a glass, darkly . . ." (1 Corinthians 13:12); that is, there is so much that is dim to us. But there we will see and understand so much more—we will continue to grow in grace and advance in knowledge.

God did not fix it so that one is born with knowledge. Instead, He gave men minds which can think and study, learn and remember. He made a world in which there is plenty to do; and through the meeting of the challenges and opportunities of this life, man develops himself and grows in character and inner strength.

God arranged it so that on this earth we would live as families. We would come to love each other. In His plan, men work together, have fellowship with one another, the strong helping the weak. We belong to each other. We would miss so much if we did not have human friendships and associations. Parents nurture and care for the little ones. Teachers impart their knowledge and help others to learn. In so many ways do we serve each other.

In this world we grow as individuals. We are born as babies and become men and women. We also grow as a people; each generation moves a bit higher in the scale of living. From all this we can know something about the place prepared for man beyond this world. I think heaven is the way it is here—only more so.

Some people think that heaven is a place where we will find eternal rest. But the idea of resting forever does not seem very exciting to me. For many it will be a blessed relief to be rid of their old, tired, patched-up, and pain-ridden bodies. But the Bible promises that in heaven we will be given a new body with which we can accomplish more.

There is a lovely verse in Revelation which says, "Blessed are the dead which die in the Lord from henceforth: Yea, saith the Spirit, that they may rest from their labors; and their works do follow them" (14:13). The key words in that verse are "labors" and "works." Here the word "labors" means weariness, suffering, exhaustion; the word "works" means results achieved and abilities that are acquired. Our wearisome burdens will be left behind; our abilities and capacities will be kept and developed.

Speaking of heaven, the Bible says, "His servants shall serve him" (Revelation 22:3). I do not know exactly what type of work we will do, but I do know it will be in God's service and that is the best work of all. Here we are so handicapped; there we will have both the abilities and the opportunities to do our best. The next life will be filled with exciting activity.

## A Place to Know One Another

In heaven we will be the same people as we are here. Our personal identities will survive. Many things about you will survive death—your temperament, your abilities, your personality. If you know someone here, you will know him when you meet him there. But fellowship one with another will be on a different basis in the next life.

Here we do not really know each other. We are too hurried to get acquainted, and we are not even capable of really knowing

ourselves. After some shameful action we say, "I don't know why
I did that"—and we don't. Certainly we are not capable of judging
others here.

On the other side of life the veil will be lifted, and because we
will know each other and understand, we will be kinder and more
patient. We will love more completely and more creatively. There
we will mean more to one another. Here we are separated by class
and color and creed; there we will all simply be children of God.

There are many people on this earth whom I admire but whom
I have never had a chance to know. I am disappointed that I never
got to see President Franklin Roosevelt. There are many others I
could name. I would like to talk with Abraham Lincoln, with Saint
Paul, David, and many others. In the next life I will have that
privilege. There I will see again and love again those who have
gone on before me. We have not lost our loved ones who have
died.

Best of all, we will see God face to face. The very thought of
being in God's presence is awe-inspiring. There are many things I
want to talk with God about. There I can do it.

## Redemption Made Complete

Not only is heaven a place where we can work and grow and be
useful, where we will have real and complete fellowship one with
another and with God; it is also a place where our redemption will
be made complete. Here we have a hard time with ourselves. We
do things we should not do, and we fail to do much that we
should. We feel shame and remorse, our consciences hurt, and we
are so often miserably defeated. There God's redemptive love and
power will complete our development.

As I have studied God's Word, I have come to realize that there
will be differences in our rewards in the next life. We will not find
monotonous uniformity or commonplace equality there. The Bible
very clearly teaches that there will be justice in the next life. I am
sure that heavenly justice will be for the purposes of redemption
rather than vengeance. Surely it is as Whittier wrote:

> I know not where His islands lift
> Their fronded palms in air;
> I only know I cannot drift
> Beyond His love and care.

There is so much about the next life that no one knows. But we do know the most important thing: we enter heaven not because of any good works or merit of ours; we enter it through the merits of Jesus Christ alone and through the salvation purchased by His blood. After we have done our best, we can only say:

> *In my hand no price I bring;*
> *Simply to Thy cross I cling.*

We remember that He promised, "Because I live, ye shall live also" (John 14:19). The details of the next life are hidden from us. But we are sure it is there, and as Richard Baxter, the English Puritan scholar, said, "Tis enough that Christ knows all, and I shall be with him."

When I think of eternal life, I think of the words our Lord said to the man who was dying by His side: "Today shalt thou be with me in paradise" (Luke 23:43). Notice those pronouns: *thou* and *me*. He was saying that they would be together and would know each other. Before I was born, my father and mother had a little girl named Ruth who died. Other children came into the home, but they always kept Ruth's picture in a little gold frame on the mantelpiece. More than once I have seen my mother or my father looking at that picture and wiping away a tear. When my father entered the City of God, I know he did not care whether they had a gate of pearl or of oak. It made no difference to him whether the streets were paved with gold or with concrete. He wanted to see little Ruth. If she had not been there, or if he had not known her, then even heaven in all its glory would have been a disappointing place to him.

I know this brings up some problems. But somehow, I also know that all of those problems are solved in heaven. I don't worry about the problems of the next life.

We remember how at the grave of Lazarus, Jesus said, "Lazarus, come forth" (John 11:43). He was Lazarus on this side; he was still Lazarus on the other side. Jesus said to Martha, "Thy brother shall rise again" (verse 23). He was her brother on this side—he was still her brother on the other side. The Greek language has no word for our word *personality*. So, in translation we talk about the resurrection of the body, and we think in terms of the physical body. In the Apostle's Creed we say, "I believe in the resurrection of the body." But really, it is the survival of the personality. This physical body of ours goes back to dust. It is the person who survives. Seeing those we love and having fellowship with them again is a glorious expectation.

At this point, however, I oftentimes find myself troubled. Also we will meet again those whom we have done wrong—those to whom we have been untruthful—those we have hurt—those to whom we have been disloyal—those to whom we have been dishonest. That is not a very comforting thought. All of us have some people we would just as soon not meet again!

In the City of God the truth will come out, and I can imagine many situations in this life in which the truth would be very painful.

On the other hand, I know that heaven is a place where all the wrongs are righted, all the sins are forgiven, and all these things in our personal relationships will somehow be straightened out and they will be all right. Thank God for that assurance and that prospect!

## Four Chapters in the Bible

There are four chapters in the Bible which especially help me in my belief in eternal life. At times I like to read these four chapters at one sitting. They firm up my own faith.

The first one is John 14. Here Jesus is speaking to His closest friends about His own leaving. They were noticeably and visibly disturbed. Here He gives them three reasons why they can have faith instead of fear:

1. "Ye believe in God" (verse 1). What a tremendous difference that makes! It means that we are in a world that was created—it did not just happen to be here. It means there is One who can handle every situation. We are not orphans; we are not alone. We believe in God.

2. "Believe also in me" (verse 1). No one of us is good enough. But we do not face eternity trusting in our own righteousness. Every one of us stands in need of a Saviour.

3. "I go to prepare a place for you" (verse 2). There is a definite place where people live after death. Where that place is, exactly what it is like, what people do there, and many other uncertainties are not really of prime importance. The important facts are that there is a place, it is God's House, it is prepared, and it is available to each and every one of us through faith in Christ. The remainder

of John 14 is a beautiful, inspiring statement to give one confidence and courage.

Then I like to read John 20. Jesus had died and had been buried. His closest loved ones were both hopeless and afraid. Then came Mary Magdalene to the tomb on Sunday morning and found the stone rolled away. She ran to tell His disciples. These disciples came and they found that the tomb was empty. But none of them thought Jesus had risen.

After the others had gone, Mary stood outside the sepulchre weeping. It was then that the Lord appeared unto her. She became sure that He was alive. That chapter also tells about how He appeared to the disciples that Sunday night, as they were trembling with fear behind closed doors. After that experience they never were afraid again. Also, the chapter tells how eight days later, He appeared again unto His disciples, and how the doubt of Thomas was taken away.

In Jerusalem today, they show two places which are claimed to be the tomb of Jesus. We are not sure which one of these is the place, but we are sure that both tombs are empty. And when I become sure of Christ's Resurrection, I have no doubt as to the fact of eternal life. There are still questions I cannot answer, but I know that He promised, "Because I live, ye shall live also" (John 14:19). I believe that.

The third chapter that I like to read is 1 Corinthians 15. To my mind, this chapter is the greatest statement of the Christian faith that has ever been made. (Of course, when I say that, I am not including the words of our Lord).

Paul begins, "I declare unto you the gospel. . . ." We all know that the word *Gospel* means "good news." Many times a preacher can preach the truth and yet not be declaring good news. For example, I may say diphtheria is a bad disease; that is true but that is not good news. The good news is that there is a vaccine that can prevent diphtheria—or a medicine that will cure diphtheria.

I may say that man is a sinner—and that is true. But that is not the good news. Or, I may say the world is bad, and I can spend every sermon I preach talking about all the bad things in the world, and I would be telling the truth. But neither would that be the good news. The Gospel is that there is One who can take a sinful person and redeem that person; or, take a bad world and make it good. That is the good news.

Next in this chapter, Paul tells us what the Gospel is. There are three main parts:

1. First, "Christ died for our sins" (verse 3). There are several things that one can say about that, but one thing is that He believed in something enough to die for it. I know there are people who feel that the Christian faith is not important, and they give very little time or attention to it. But, then let us remember the Son of God believed that it was important enough to die for it. Most important, some mighty deed was accomplished that day on Calvary. Something was done that forever makes a difference in man's relationship with God and God's relationship with man. No one of us can explain it. It goes beyond human understanding, but by faith we can accept it.

2. The second point of the Christian Gospel Paul makes is ". . . he rose again the third day . . ." (verse 4). Man had done his worst. We remember the betrayal at Gethsemane, the shameful trials, the march to Calvary, the nails being driven into His flesh, the ridicule, and His death. We know that He was buried in a tomb, and that the tomb was sealed with a large stone. We know that around that tomb was placed a guard of Roman soldiers.

Then God took over. The earth began to shake, those soldiers became as dead men, an angel came and rolled away the stone, and the Lord, Jesus Christ, came walking out of that tomb into the sunshine.

I have visited the place where John Wesley, the founder of the Methodist church, is buried. But nobody can visit the place where Jesus is buried. He is not buried anywhere. He is still alive!

3. Then the third point of the Christian Gospel is: We, too, shall live. Paul triumphantly declares, "But thanks be to God, which giveth us the victory through our Lord Jesus Christ" (verse 57). Our lives are not going to end up in a ditch in some cemetery.

The fourth chapter I like to read is Revelation 21. John was exiled to the Isle of Patmos. He had been faithful and patient so long that God pulled back the curtain and let him look over into the other side. Earlier I mentioned how he saw "there was no more sea." In this chapter I especially like to read the fourth verse. It has a melody that thrills the human soul: "And God shall wipe away all tears from their eyes; and there shall be no more death, neither sorrow, nor crying, neither shall there be any more pain: for the former things are passed away."

# 4

# *The Fourth Spiritual Wonder:*

# The Privilege
# of Prayer

Often people write or speak to me of problems for which I just do not know the answers. In such cases I admit that I do not know how to advise him or her, but I suggest that we enter into a compact together to pray about it. Many times, as a result of our prayers, problems have been solved.

One man, however, in response to my prayer suggestion, wrote back a very difficult letter. "Before I agree to pray," he wrote, "answer the following five questions: What is prayer? Can anybody pray? Can you prove the value of prayer? How does one pray? What results can I expect from prayer?" How would you answer those questions? Let's take them one at a time:

## What Is Prayer?

What is prayer? One night I heard a very fine speech by a scientist who explained that many people think of religion as some form of magic which they can use for their own benefit. But prayer is not magic. Prayer is very much within the laws of the universe, and the spiritual laws of the universe are as certain and sure as are the physical laws. Physical and spiritual laws work together; they are never in conflict. As Pierhal states it, "Although prayer is supernatural, it is not antinatural."

Prayer is never a substitute for effort. A certain schoolboy failed in his examinations. He was very much surprised. When the teacher inquired how much he had studied, he replied, "I did not study at all. I thought that if you asked God to help you, that was all you had to do."

On the other hand, prayer is something beyond our efforts. On the night of July 10, 1943, General Dwight D. Eisenhower watched the vast armada of 3,000 ships sailing across from Malta to the shores of Sicily for a great battle. The General saluted his heroic men and then bowed his head in prayer. To an officer beside him, Eisenhower explained, "There comes a time when you've used your brains, your training, your technical skill, and the die is cast and the events are in the hands of God, and there you have to leave them."

Prayer is need finding a voice—embarrassment seeking relief—a friend in search of a Friend—knocking on a barred door—reaching out through the darkness. Prayer is speaking, or thinking, or feeling with the belief that there is Somebody who hears and who cares and who will respond. Prayer is a means of contact with God. Prayer is opening our lives to the purposes of God.

Prayer is not a method of using God; rather prayer is a means of reporting for duty to God.

## Can Anybody Pray?

Can anybody pray? The answer is that everybody can and does pray. Some people think they are self-sufficient and do not need help. Some people scoff at the value of prayer, calling it a silly waste of time. Some people lack faith; others are ashamed to face God in prayer because they do not want God telling them what to do.

But at one time or another, in one kind of crisis or another, everybody prays. Need becomes stronger than doubt and sometimes we will turn to God in spite of ourselves. There is a hidden hunger of man's spiritual self that cries out to be satisfied. Sooner or later that hidden hunger asserts itself and makes its demands felt. It is as Victor Hugo said, "There are times in a man's life when, regardless of the attitude of the body, the soul is on its knees in prayer."

## Can You Prove the Value of Prayer?

Can you prove the value of prayer? By various tests, many have sought to demonstrate that prayer gets results. But I have never been too interested in such experiments. I am not sure that prayer values can be proved, but certainly they can be known. There is a difference. In fact, anyone who sincerely prays is himself a proof of prayer.

About prayer, Abraham Lincoln once said: "I have had so many evidences of His direction, so many instances of times when I have been controlled by some other power than my own will, that I cannot doubt that this power comes from God. I frequently see my way clear to a decision when I am conscious that I have not sufficient facts on which to found it. I am satisfied that, when the Almighty wants me to do, or not to do, a particular thing, He finds a way of letting me know. I talk to God and when I do, my mind seems relieved and a way is suggested." I doubt if Lincoln ever tried to prove the value of prayer—but he knew it.

## How Do I Pray?

How does one pray? Late one night my doorbell rang. When I opened the door I found a man standing there. He said, "Something happened to me tonight that caused me to want to pray. But I have never prayed in my life and I do not know how. I don't want you to pray for me—I want you to teach me how to pray for myself." We talked for a while and I found he had never been to church except for a few times when he was a child. He had never read the Bible. I asked if he knew the Lord's Prayer. He asked, "What is that?"

I told him about Jesus' disciples asking Him to teach them to pray. In response, He gave them a short prayer. I gave my visitor a New Testament and marked the place. I told him that every time he wanted to pray he should get down on his knees, open the Testament, and read that prayer aloud. He said he would do that and he was deeply in earnest. As a result, that man had a really remarkable religious experience and has developed a wonderful faith.

The best way I know to learn to pray is to learn the Lord's Prayer by heart. It is easy to commit the Lord's Prayer to memory; it takes time and persistence to learn it by heart. But when those words that Jesus gave come out of our own hearts, then we are truly praying.

## What Results Can I Expect From Prayer?

What results can be expected from prayer? Some years ago, four people who knew much about prayer joined together in forming a declaration. They were George Washington Carver, Glenn Frank, Rufus Jones, and Muriel Lester. They wrote:

> Sometimes a bridge falls, but that does not mean that the law of gravity has failed. Sometimes lines are short-circuited, but that does not mean that the law of electricity has failed. And sometimes a disciple betrays his Lord, but that does not mean that the law of love has failed. Sometimes a prayer is not answered, but that does not mean that the power of prayer has failed. The scientist does not quit when the lights are short-circuited, nor when the bridge falls. Then why should we? Just think of what would happen if all church people united in prayer with as great faith in the laws of God as scientists have in the laws of nature.
>
> Science is showing us that the smaller and more invisible a thing is, the more powerful it is. Pasteur proved to an unbelieving world that bacteria ten thousand times smaller than a flea could kill a man. Physicists are proving that the tiny cosmic ray is far more potent and penetrating than the visible sun ray. Radio operators are proving that the short wavelength carries a message farther than the long wavelength. And love is invisible, but all-powerful love is more potent and penetrating than cannons, submarines or airplanes ever can be. Prayer in the inner room, invisible to the eyes of men, is still as potent as in the days when Jesus said, "Pray to thy Father which is in secret; and thy Father which seeth in secret shall reward thee openly."

English poet George Meredith said, "Who riseth from prayer a better man, his prayer is answered." That is really the best result of prayer, but prayer brings definite and tangible results. However, we must keep in mind that we ourselves must become part of the answer.

A poor man who lived in the country broke his leg in an accident. That meant he was laid up for a long while, unable to work. His family was large and needed help. Someone got up a prayer meeting at the church to pray for this family. While the people were praying and asking God to help the family, there was a loud knock on the door of their home. Someone tiptoed to the door, opened it, and there stood a young farm boy who said, "My dad could not attend the prayer meeting tonight, so he just sent his prayers in a wagon." And there was the wagon loaded with meat, potatoes, apples, and other things from the farm.

We must become part of the answer to our prayers, but only part. God adds to our abilities, opportunities, and resources whatever is needed and is right to bring about the full answer. It is as Tennyson said:

> More things are wrought by prayer
> Than this world dreams of. . . .

## Learn to Pray

The lights were burning, the janitor was running the vacuum cleaner, and the organist was playing a beautiful melody as I walked into my church one morning. Into the building some electric wires run, over which flows that marvelous power that gives light, that cleans up dirt, and produces harmony.

Now, the God who created electricity did not forget to create a power that will do those same things for a life—and the channel through which that power flows is what we call prayer. It is the only thing Jesus' disciples ever asked Him to teach them. They knew that once they learned to pray, the power of God was at their disposal.

In response to their request, Christ gave them seven simple steps to follow. He needed only sixty-six words (Matthew 6:9–13), and the power of God is available to any who follow those steps.

1. Start by thinking of God. Forget about your own needs and problems for the time being and saturate your mind with thoughts of God. This will silence the mind and bring relaxation. Think of Him as "Our Father which art in heaven." You cannot imagine a cyclone in heaven. Heaven suggests calmness, beauty, and rest. Note the first word is "Our." You cannot pray for yourself alone.

2. Then let your prayer begin with thanking God for what He has done for you. Think of some definite blessings you have received and "name them one by one." You cannot hope to name them all, but do at least name some. This will lead you to positive and constructive thinking. It tends to diminish bitterness, disappointment, and defeatist attitudes. "Hallowed be Thy name."

3. Naturally, the next step is consecration—"Thy kingdom come, thy will be done." As we think of the benefits we have received from God, we want Him more and more in our lives and in our world. As we realize that it is better for us to have God, we increasingly want Him to have full possession of us. And when God possesses us, we want to help Him possess the world about us. So we pray that God will use us in His work. We begin to see things we might do to help, and we gladly commit ourselves to those opportunities. Anything that we can do to bring in His Kingdom we become willing and eager to do.

4. As you realize the greatness of God, you understand that all we have comes from His hand. If God stopped giving for even one minute, every bit of life on earth would cease. We think of our complete dependence on Him. So we pray, "Give us this day our daily bread," which is the title of a poem by Maltbie D. Babcock:

> Back of the loaf is the snowy flour,
>   And back of the flour is the mill,
> And back of the mill is the wheat, and the shower,
>   And the sun and the Father's will.

5. Then, when we realize we are utterly dependent upon God, but that wrong within our own lives blocks out our ability to serve, confession comes next. "Forgive us our sins" is the fifth step. Here we need to be specific. In dealing with many people, I have come to see that it is usually some specific wrong that needs to be settled. When we become willing to turn loose "that one thing," we usually have little difficulty in settling all the other things that are wrong.

6. As we seek forgiveness of our own sins we are simultaneously seeking the forgiveness of every other person. Because as God comes into our own hearts there also comes in a deep and abiding love for Him and for all other people. Here we feel the "expulsive power of a new affection." Prejudice, jealousy, hate, grudges, and indifference cannot live in a heart into which God has come. Thus it is easy and natural to pray, "As we forgive others."

7. Finally comes the most important step of all. It is "Amen." That is a big and strong word. Literally, it means, "So let it be." It is a resolve of honesty. Obviously it would be dishonest and unfair to ask God to do for us what we are unwilling to do for ourselves.

That word "Amen" is a promise that you will do all within your own power to answer your prayer.

Also, "Amen" means the same thing Jesus meant when He said, "Into thy hands I commend my spirit." That is, I have done my best and now I am willing to leave the results to God. It is a pledge of faith and confidence. Thus, when one has prayed, his mind can be at rest in the assurance that God has heard and will answer.

Those seven simple steps are the "how" of prayer and, when honestly taken, they become the pathway to power—power that gives light and understanding, a clean heart, and harmony within the soul.

## The Lord's Prayer

> After this manner therefore pray ye: Our Father which
> art in heaven, Hallowed by thy name.
> Thy kingdom come. Thy will be done in earth, as it is in
> heaven.
> Give us this day our daily bread.
> And forgive us our debts, as we forgive our debtors.
> And lead us not into temptation, but deliver us from
> evil:
> For thine is the kingdom, and the power, and the glory,
> for ever. Amen (Matthew 6:9–13).

The Lord's Prayer is recorded twice in the Gospels. In Luke's account (Luke 11:1–4), we have the disciples saying to Jesus, "Lord, teach us to pray. . . ." It is important to note that this is the only thing the disciples ever asked the Lord to teach them. They never asked Him to teach them how to perform miracles, how to organize churches, or even how to win the world. After they had seen Jesus praying, they realized that once they learned how to pray, all of these other things would come.

We know that the Sermon on the Mount is really the "set of instructions" for the disciples, and as we read this sermon we find no section teaching the disciples any of the other activities in which they would be engaged, except that of praying. Instead of giving them a lengthy discourse on the techniques of prayer, the Lord simply gave them a prayer.

Really, the Lord's Prayer is a pattern to follow, and as one prays within that framework he will find himself taking hold of the power of God. If you want to experience this power, get somewhere where it is quiet and you will not be disturbed. Then take the Lord's Prayer and begin to read those words very slowly. Think about what each word is saying, and let each word stimulate your thinking. Then express in your own words the thoughts that come to you as you think the words of the Lord's Prayer. This is something I do frequently, and I find that my thoughts are stimulated in many ways by the Lord's Prayer. I really think the Lord's Prayer should be the basis of prolonged meditation on the part of all Christian people.

"Our Father which art in heaven"—the first step in prayer is not asking for something, but silencing the mind: "Be still, and know that I am God" (Psalms 46:10). My own father was buried in Westview Cemetery in Atlanta, Georgia. Afterwards, I was a minister in that city for twelve years, and during those years, I went to that cemetery many times for funeral services. Almost without exception, after we had concluded the service, I would drive by the grave of my father, get out of my car, and just stand there for a little while. I would think about him, and many memories would crowd my mind. I would think of his character, of his goodness, of his kindness, of his love for me. That experience always left me inspired and lifted up. So, when I begin to pray, I just like to stop and think about my heavenly Father. I think of His goodness, and His purposes, and His love for me. The beginning of prayer is centering our minds on God.

"Which art in heaven"—that does not mean that God is sitting down in some far-off place of golden streets and pearly gates. What Jesus had in mind was the whole creation, the entire universe. In fact, I think the better translation would be: "Who art in the universe." God is everywhere in His universe, creating, upholding it, and carrying it forward. God is where we are, and we are a part of His creative purpose. We are being undergirded by His wisdom and His love. However, as I pray these words, I like to think of John's vision of heaven as recorded in chapter 21 of the Book of Revelation. He depicts heaven as a place where "God shall wipe away all tears from their eyes; and there shall be no more death, neither sorrow, nor crying, neither shall there be any more pain . . ." (verse 4). That is such a beautiful and peaceful scene. One cannot imagine a cyclone in heaven, or an earthquake, or an automobile wreck, or a war, or any of the things that bring sorrow and pain to human life. As I think of God in this way, I feel calm in my own soul.

"Hallowed be thy name"—thinking of God, I feel that He is exalted above all things on the earth. At this part of the prayer, one is moved to think of the words of the great hymn:

> Holy, holy, holy! Lord, God Almighty!
> Early in the morning, our song shall rise to Thee!

We feel that the name of God is almost too sacred to be spoken by human lips. As we feel His presence, our hearts are filled with awe, and our ego is melted into deep reverence. At this point, our faith becomes greatly strengthened.

One of the Ten Commandments forbids the taking of the name of the Lord in vain. We generally think of that in reference to profanity, but actually the most profane word a Christian can utter is "hopeless." The psalmist repeats one question twice in the same psalm; it is this: "Why art thou cast down, O my soul? and why art thou disquieted in me?" Then, the psalmist says, "Hope thou in God . . ." (Psalms 42:5). The point is, when one believes in God and has God in his life, he has strength and faith. The more reverent our attitude toward God, the stronger we are inside.

"Thy kingdom come"—since we began our prayer with God, we continue to think of God as we pray. Thus, our prayer is not *my* kingdom come, but *Thy* Kingdom come. So many times, the reason one prays is that he wants something from God, or wants God to do something, and his prayers are literally selfish. But, when one's mind is filled with God, he begins to think in terms of what God wants. He begins to pray for a society in which God would feel at home. He thinks of all the things in our society that hurt, and he suddenly wants all those things eliminated from our world.

Have you ever been in a group when someone said, "Let us repeat together the Lord's Prayer"? That is the tragedy—we sometimes simply *repeat* instead of pray. It does not take much effort to say "thy kingdom come," but praying those words can shake us to our very foundations.

"Thy will be done"—here again, we forget our own desires, and we put our minds upon what His desire is. All too often, what this prayer means to many people is a negative acceptance of pain, defeat, and suffering. We associate these words with our Lord's praying in Gethsemane, "Thy will be done." And then we think about His going from Gethsemane to Calvary's cross. For many of us, "God's will" and "the cross" have become synonymous terms. But, just as you will life and joy and success for your children, so God wills for His children.

"In earth, as it is in heaven"—as we picture heaven, we picture a life completely in harmony with God. We cannot think of disobedience in heaven.

"Give us this day our daily bread"—some of the Bible commentaries seek to spiritualize this particular petition, and try to make it mean the same thing as Jesus meant when He said, "I am the bread of life . . ." (John 6:35). These words can be taken literally and can be applied to the actual physical needs of our life. We do have souls; but we also have physical bodies, and those physical bodies must be maintained. We have every right to ask our heavenly Father for the material needs of our lives. It is not wrong for me to ask God to help me make my business succeed, or to help me get a raise in my pay. God understands when we are burdened by debts and by the lack of things that we really need. I would hate to think that my children ever reached the place that they hesitated to talk with me about the physical needs of their lives, and our heavenly Father is just as concerned with His children.

At this point, it is well to note the pronouns that Jesus uses in this prayer: "*Our* father" . . . "*our* daily bread" . . . "*our* trespasses" . . . "lead *us* not into temptation." We are taught here that our prayers can never involve just ourselves alone. We cannot really pray unless we include our fellow men. In prayer, we recognize our membership in the family of God. Lloyd C. Douglas said it beautifully in *The Big Fisherman*: "My own opinion of the mysterious Nazarene is difficult to define. On first sight of Him, I was a bit disappointed. He is not an heroic figure, but the man has a compelling voice. I can't describe it or the effect of it. It is a unifying voice that converts a great crowd of mutually distrustful strangers into a tight little group of blood relatives."

"And forgive us our debts" (sins, trespasses)—as we think of God, His glory, His goodness, His greatness; as we think of His Kingdom on earth, and His perfect will; as we think of our complete dependence upon Him, then naturally we come to confession. "Forgive us" comes readily to our lips. We think of the many wrongs we have done. In His presence, we want no stains on our lives, no sins in our hearts. Having the Spirit of God firmly implanted in our consciousness as we have been praying to this point, we become more sure of God's willingness to forgive.

Many years ago, I heard an evangelist tell a story about a boy he saw riding on a train one day. The boy kept looking out the window and nervously rolling the brim of his hat. The preacher asked him what the trouble was, and the boy told him how he had run away from home, vowing he would never go back. But the world did not welcome him as he thought it would. He couldn't find a job, and he ran out of money. In desperation he wrote his father, asking if he would be welcome back home. His home was on the outskirts of a little town, and the boy said that he would be passing through on the train on a certain day, and that, if he were welcome at home, would his father please hang a towel on the front gate. If there were no towel, then the boy would not get off the train and would go on. As they neared the little town, the boy said to the preacher, "You look. I'm afraid to." The preacher looked out and saw not only a towel hanging on the post, but towels and sheets waving from the limbs of all the trees! He told the boy to look for himself. When the boy saw the welcome signs, he grabbed his old suitcase, put it under his arm, jumped off the train before it stopped, and ran down the dusty road toward his father's welcome. We are so conscious and ashamed of our sins. But when we think of God and see Him, we are ready and eager to rush back into His arms.

"As we forgive our debtors" ("those who trespass against us")—recognizing our own need of forgiveness, and wanting a restored fellowship with the heavenly Father, it becomes easier to forgive those who have done us wrong. One of the most helpful experiences in prayer is to substitute the name of a particular person in this petition: "Forgive me as I forgive_____." As I pray this prayer, a name comes before me. Let me keep praying until that name is clear in my own mind and in my own heart.

"And lead us not into temptation, but deliver us from evil"—this is a recognition of our own weakness. Many people think of all the bad things that might happen, and worry about what they would do if those things should happen. When we think of sorrows, losses, illnesses, and all the tragedies of life, we worry that we will not have strength to stand before them. So often, when some heavy burden falls upon us, we find that we have strength we did not know we had, and we can "walk through the valley."

Curiously, when we think of temptations and wrongs that might confront us, we have confidence to feel that we can handle them, and that we can walk with temptation without being hurt. Often it happens, when the temptation comes, that we discover weaknesses we did not know we had. So it is that trials bring out our strengths, and temptations uncover our weaknesses.

As we contemplate God and His strength, we become aware of our own inabilities, and we recognize our need for His help. Having been forgiven, we do not want to sin again. This is a prayer not only for strength in time of temptation, but also for escape from temptation. It is as John Ruskin expressed it: "No one can ask honestly or happily to be delivered from temptation unless he has honestly and firmly determined to do the best he can to keep out of it." Furthermore, this is a prayer that we may never become a temptation to someone else. In *Measure for Measure*, Shakespeare asked a very searching question: "The temptor or the tempted, who sins most?" Here is a question that can well occupy our minds.

"For thine is the kingdom, and the power, and the glory, for ever"—in some of the manuscripts, this phrase is omitted, but what a grand climax it is to the prayer! It ends our prayer where we began—centered in God. It is right and proper to pray for our own needs—for guidance, bread, forgiveness, strength—but our needs are never the beginning nor the end. The glory belongs to God. We never pray with only our own good in mind. "Thine is the kingdom" means that I accord to the King my disciplined obedience. "Thine is the power" means that I am not afraid, because God is able and sufficient in every situation. "Thine is the glory" means that I am not seeking glory for myself. "For ever" means that my horizon is lifted even beyond the bounds of time, and I know that God is for eternity.

"Amen"—this is one of the most important petitions of any prayer. We recall that when our Lord was hanging from the cross, He lifted His eyes and said, "Father, into thy hands I commend my spirit . . ." (Luke 23:46). He had now given His best, and He was willing to entrust it all to the hands of God. The word *amen* means faith in God; it means a willingness to trust His will and His judgment and His power. The word *amen* brings to one a sense of deep confidence and relief.

## Pray Until You Get the Answer

Someone once asked me this question: "Jesus said, 'Ask and it shall be given thee.' How many times should I pray for something?"

Jesus answered that question with a story about a man who had an unexpected guest at midnight. Custom required that he serve his guest but, as it was with "Old Mother Hubbard," his cupboard was bare.

At midnight there were no stores open where he could buy some food. So he went over to his neighbor's door and started knocking. From inside came a sleepy voice saying, "Trouble me not: the door is now shut, and my children are with me in bed; I cannot rise and give to thee."

I sympathize with the neighbor. It was dark and he had no convenient light switch as we have. To make a light was considerable trouble. The fire was out, and it is never pleasant to get out of a warm bed in a cold house. And doubtless he had had trouble getting the children to sleep. If he got up, likely they would awaken and it would be a problem getting them back to sleep.

The man outside, however, kept on knocking until finally his neighbor got up and gave to him, "because of his importunity." *Importunity* means persistence, to keep on. Then to this story Jesus adds, "Ask, and it shall be given you; seek, and ye shall find; knock, and it shall be opened unto you."

Jesus does not mean that God is like the reluctant neighbor. Instead, what He would have us understand is that if a man would answer a request merely to keep from being bothered further, how much more will God answer our requests of Him. But the secret of power in prayer is persistence.

We make frequent requests of God, but before our requests become real prayers we must, even as the friend at midnight, come in the spirit of urgent need. We must remember that Heaven only hears what we are determined it shall hear. God is not a trifler, He is completely in earnest, and He does not hear us until we become tireless in our determination.

We remember how Jacob wrestled with his "angel" saying, "I will not let thee go, except thou bless me" (Genesis 32:26). Jesus told His disciples, "Tarry ye in the city of Jerusalem, until ye be endued with power from on high" (Luke 24:49). Note the words "tarry . . . until." Before Paul received the grace sufficient for the thorn in his flesh, he prayed three times (2 Corinthians 12:8). For other things he might have prayed three hundred times because he tells us he prayed "without ceasing" (Romans 1:9). Jesus prayed until, "His sweat was as it were great drops of blood falling down to the ground" (Luke 22:44).

How many times should I pray for something? Until the answer comes! As our forefathers used to say, "until you pray it through."

## Prayer Changes Things—Even You!

A mother said to me, "When my boy went away to the battlefield, I prayed that God would keep him safe. I was persistent in my praying, not just once did I ask or just once a day. It was my constant prayer all day long every day. But he was killed. I asked, but God did not answer."

My reply is that God did hear her prayer and that He did have the power to keep her boy safe. God could change the course of bullets in their flight if He chose to. God answers prayer. So obviously, keeping that boy safe was not His answer. The thing this mother must do is to keep on praying until she does get God's answer. God answers at the proper time in the proper way, and it is not ours to question how and when, it is ours to pray until the answer comes.

Jesus tells us that "men ought always to pray, and not to faint" (Luke 18:1). To faint means to quit. One can allow bitterness, or disappointment, or lack of understanding, or hopelessness to turn him away from God. And though God's answer may be better than anything we had dreamed of, because we have turned from Him, we fail to get the answer and thereby miss the supreme blessing of life for us.

Persistent prayer does two things: it changes the course of events, and second, it changes us. Our world is not a rigid, fixed, mechanical thing. It is a spiritual universe, governed by powerful forces far beyond the present understanding of mankind. Jesus so understood the governing forces of the world that He could speak to the winds and waves and they obeyed His voice. He could heal sickness in a moment's flash, He could make the blind see, the crippled walk, even the dead live.

Certainly we do not understand the higher spiritual forces which have the power to change even our physical world. But we do not have to understand this power to use it. We might not know what electricity is, where it comes from, or how it is made. Nevertheless, we use it to light up our homes, run our factories, and provide us power in a thousand other ways. Marconi, who invented the radio, told a friend that there was one thing he did not understand about it and that was "why it works."

Before the first H-bomb was built, scientists told us about atomic power. Because we believed that power existed and that it could be harnessed, we spent millions of dollars to develop it. Scientists are also telling us about spiritual power. Renowned electrical engineer Charles Steinmetz said, "The greatest discoveries in the next fifty years will be in the realm of the spiritual." Dr. J. B. Rhine has stated, "As a result of thousands of experimental trials we found it to be a fact that the mind has a force that can act on matter." And when the mind of man meets the mind of God through the medium of prayer, something happens. Prayer changes things. So, instead of fainting, we ought to keep on praying until the change does come.

## "No" Is Not the Final Answer

Jesus tells us, "Your Father knoweth what things ye have need of, before ye ask him" (Matthew 6:8). So why should we persistently keep on asking Him? Because frequently God's answer must be delayed until we are ready to receive it. Not only does persistent prayer set in motion spiritual forces in our world, also it works changes within ourselves.

Elizabeth Barrett Browning tells us, "Every wish, with God, is a prayer," but frequently our wishes need to be cleansed and purified. It is true that God "knoweth what things we have need of," but it is just as true that often we ourselves do not know. We just think we know and mercifully God withholds an answer until we come up with the right request. It is often said that *no* is an answer, but *no* is never the *final* answer. God has for us a glorious *yes*, and we must keep on asking until that *yes* comes. To merely accept God's *no* is to accept defeat.

Paul asked God for the chance to preach in Bythinia. God said *no*, but Paul kept on asking until he got a *yes*. The *yes* was to go into Macedonia. There Paul did his greatest work. If he had stopped on the *no*, we would never have heard of him. Edison received a thousand *no* answers to his efforts to find the secret of the light bulb. But he kept on trying until the *yes* came.

If God says no to our prayer, it does not mean we should stop praying. It means that we keep praying until we find the prayer to which He can say yes. The supreme object of prayer is not the attainment of some desire, but rather is it to know God. Knowing God, we know His purposes and knowing His purposes, we desire them above our own. And desiring His purposes, it then becomes safe for God to entrust us with His power. But God will not give us His power for unworthy uses.

Jacob once prayed that if God would do whatever he asked and give him whatever he wanted, then he would support God's work and give Him a tenth of his income. (*See* Genesis 28:20–22.) That is mere childish bargaining, yet we pray the same way. "Lord, if you will make me well I will go to church." "If you will look after my son on the battlefield, I will live a good life." "If you will help me to get more money, I will give you a tithe." To that sort of praying God says no.

Jacob kept on praying and one morning after wrestling all night with God in prayer, he prayed, "Tell me, I pray thee, thy name." To know a name was to know the person. So Jacob's persistence led him to the supreme prayer, "Reveal thyself to me." God answered with a glorious yes. Jacob forgets the bargains he wanted to make, he is not thinking of what he can get out of God, but with humility and reverence, he says, "I have seen God face to face."

Suppose you could go into a room where Jesus was sitting. What would you do? Would you give Him a list of all the things you want, as children give to Santa Claus? Would you ask Him the explanation of a dozen problems you have been unable to solve? No—you would fall on your knees, you would kiss the hem of His garment, and being with Him, all your desires would be satisfied. That is where we get to when we keep on praying " 'til we pray it through."

## Your Prayer Will Be Answered

We have the promise of God: "Call unto me, and I will answer thee" (Jeremiah 33:3). Jesus emphasized the fact that God keeps that promise. He said, "Ask, and it shall be given you" (Matthew 7:7). He said, "All things, whatsoever ye shall ask in prayer, believing, ye shall receive" (Matthew 21:22). He said, "If two of you shall agree on earth as touching any thing that they shall ask, it shall be done for them of my Father" (Matthew 18:19).

Yet, right in the Bible we find many prayers where it seems God did not answer. Moses prayed to enter the Promised Land, but his request was refused and he died. The psalmist said, "Oh my God, I cry in the daytime, but thou hearest not" (Psalms 22:2). In Lamentations 3:44 we read, "Thou covered thyself with a cloud, that our prayer should not pass through." Habakkuk 1:2 asks, "O Lord, how long shall I cry, and thou wilt not hear!" Paul asked that a "thorn in the flesh" which handicapped his work be removed, but his prayer request was not granted (2 Corinthians 12:9). Even Christ prayed "Let this cup pass from me," but He drank its bitter dregs.

There are many people today who have lost faith because when they called unto God they seemed to receive no answer. They have even felt that their prayers went unheard, that they were just speaking words out into space. What, then, is the answer for the problem of unanswered prayer?

The fault may be in us. Remember that Jesus warned us that if we refuse to forgive others, God will not forgive us (Matthew 6:15). And the psalmist says, "If I regard iniquity in my heart, the Lord will not hear me" (Psalms 66:18). James says, "Ye ask, and receive not, because ye ask amiss" (James 4:3).

Because of our own refusal to do ourselves what we ask God to do, because of our refusal to face the sin of our own lives, because of asking for the wrong reasons, we do not get the answer we ask for. The first prayer, and the beginning of every prayer, should be "Search me, O God, and know my heart: try me, and know my thoughts" (Psalms 139:23). God makes the sun to shine, but if the window in our house is dirty, God will not make the sun come through. The darkness in your room may not be a cause for asking God to make the sunshine brighter. Rather it may be a cause for you to wash your windows.

The darkness of your soul, the littleness which you have received, and the confusion in which you live may not be because God has not answered; it may be because you are unwilling to receive. God has two kinds of gifts for us. First, there are the gifts he gives whether we ask for them or not—the sun which shines, the air we breathe, the fertility in the soil. Parents give to their children such things as food, shelter, clothing, and watchful care whether the child asks for them or not.

Second, there are gifts that are given only if we ask for them. I want my son to have a college education, but I cannot give it to him unless he asks for it and wants it. If I make available for him the money he needs, he must cooperate by opening his mind through study in order to receive the education. Yes, the reason we do not receive the answers to our prayers may be in us.

## Three Possible Answers

When we make a request to God through prayer, we must remember there are three possible answers we might receive. They are: yes, no, or wait.

Frequently God's answer to our prayers is an immediate yes. Sometimes He must say no. Jesus once said to a mother, "Ye know not what ye ask" (Matthew 20:22). When my son was nine years old, he asked me repeatedly to buy him a rifle "that shoots real bullets." I think it was better for him and I am sure it was better for the rest of the family and for our neighbors for me to say no.

Most often God says no in order to say yes to something better. At the end of my second year in college I sought to get a job teaching school. I did not have the money to go to college the next year, and I was almost desperate. The choice in one school was between me and another man and I prayed that they would elect me. Instead, they elected the other man and I felt God had refused to answer my prayer.

A little later I got a letter from Dr. Snyder at Wofford College opening the way for me to go there and I went. Now as I look back I see that God's *no* to my prayer was the best answer I could have received. I probably would have been a miserable failure as a school teacher, my college work was not interrupted, and the next summer the way was opened for me to enter the ministry, which was what I really wanted.

Nearly all of us have had the experience of praying for some person to be kept safe or to be made well and yet that person died. At such times there comes over us a feeling of being forsaken. Yet I am sure that the greatest blessing even God can give is the blessing of death. To deny one the privilege of dying is to deny the privilege of living with God in the Father's House.

I prayed recently for a young mother to live. Her two children needed her so badly, yet she died. Parents have prayed for their children and yet they died. Often we cannot understand why God says no, but there will come a time when we will understand. As Paul said, "For now we see through a glass, darkly; but then face to face: now I know in part; but then shall I know even as also I am known" (1 Corinthians 13:12).

Until our prayers are answered, we must have faith. Faith means trusting where we cannot see. If everything were completely clear to us, we would not need faith and whatever God's answer to our prayer is, we must remember "the judgments of the Lord are true and righteous altogether" (Psalms 19:9).

Frequently God's answer to our prayer is *wait*. We remember how Jacob asked God for a favor and in return Jacob promised to give gifts to God. Later on, as Jacob wrestled with the angel, he forgot what he wanted God to do, instead he wanted God. He says, "I will not let thee go, except thou bless me" (Genesis 32:26). That night Jacob received the greatest blessing of his life. He says, "I have seen God face to face" (Genesis 32:30).

Too often we are so concerned about the gift that we forget to seek the Giver, and God may withhold the things we pray for if those things keep us from seeing Him. In fact, I think God may take away some of the things He has given already because we put those things before Him.

Asking for things and for favors from God is really the least important purpose of prayer. Jesus told His disciples to first pray "Our Father." Getting to know God is better than things we might ask for. The main object of prayer is to glorify Him. If you would learn to pray, study the Psalms. For the most part they are the prayers of a people in poverty, yet they almost never asked for things.

"Bless the Lord, O my soul; and all that is within me, bless his holy name"—"The Lord reigneth; let the earth rejoice"—"O give thanks unto the Lord; for he is good"—"Teach me, O Lord, the way of thy statutes; and I shall keep thy law; yea, I shall observe it with my whole heart"—"Let the words of my mouth and the meditation of my heart be acceptable in thy sight, O Lord, my strength and my redeemer."

Praise, thanksgiving, consecration and communion—those are the prayers that bring the greatest blessings to our lives. It is not wrong to want things and to ask for them. God made everything there is. But the mere possession of things does not satisfy our souls. The removing from our hearts of selfish and unholy desires by the indwelling of His Spirit is a wonderful answer to prayer. As George Meredith, in his novel *The Ordeal of Richard Feverel*, said, "Who rises from prayer a better man, his prayer is answered."

Also, we must remember that part of the answer to our prayers must be made by us. Augustine said, "Without God, we cannot. Without us, God will not." God gives the wheat, but man must till the soil, sow, reap, grind into flour, and bake if he would eat the bread.

When the children of Israel came to the Red Sea, Moses went aside to pray. In answer God said, "Speak unto the children of Israel, that they go forward" (Exodus 14:15). God said that He had done all that He needed to do. Now they must do what they could do. Sometimes God's answer to us is wisdom sufficient for us to know what we should do, sometimes it is strength sufficient for us to walk, sometimes it is inspiration to cause us to use what He has already given us.

When the final record is written, God will see that no prayers were left unanswered.

## Unanswered Prayers

Prayer is the subject of more letters that come to me than any other subject. Many people write requests for prayer, many ask how they should pray in regard to a particular situation, many ask why they have not had an answer to some specific prayer. Often someone writes, "The Bible says, 'Ask, and it shall be given you.' I have asked but it has not been given me."

Many whose prayers are not answered are bitter and resentful. They wonder if God plays favorites and hears only certain ones. Many are confused and frustrated. They have prayed and now they do not know which way to turn.

In reply, I want to say that, first, God does hear and answer prayer. In his poem "The Cotter's Saturday Night," Robert Burns said, "They never sought in vain that sought the Lord aright!" Underscore that word *aright*—that is the key. The Bible tells us, "Ye ask, and receive not, because ye ask amiss . . ." (James 4:3). As I read the Bible I find many causes of unanswered prayer. Look at some of the more common ones:

"And ye returned and wept before the Lord; but the Lord would not hearken to your voice, nor give ear unto you" (Deuteronomy 1:45). Through His servant Joshua, God had told the people what to do, but they paid no attention and did as they pleased. God's later refusal to hear their prayers was the result of their disobedience. One condition of prayer is our willingness to obey God in our lives.

Jeremiah 29:13 tells us: "And ye shall seek me, and find me, when ye shall search for me with all your heart." Half-heartedness is another cause of unanswered prayer. If we are not entirely dedicated to our own prayers, we should not expect God to waste time with us.

The Bible tells us, "If I regard iniquity in my heart, the Lord will not hear me" (Psalms 66:18). That does not mean that one must be perfect in order to pray. Surely even the vilest can pray. It does mean that we must abhor evil; that the desire of our hearts is to live right.

"But let him ask in faith, nothing wavering. . . . A double-minded man is unstable in all his ways" (James 1:6, 8). Stability is required of one who would pray. Our minds and hearts must have a fixed purpose and we must hold steadfastly to that purpose.

By far, the main reason for unanswered prayers is that our prayers are not within the will of God. Our Lord was careful to add to His prayer, ". . . nevertheless, not my will, but thine, be done" (Luke 22:42). We do not have full understanding; and even though one is completely sincere, from God's view it may be clearly seen that his prayer is not best. Our faith must be such that we trust Him with the answer. Let us ever be mindful that our larger prayer is that we be fully surrendered to God's will.

## Three Essentials for Prayer

It has been beautifully said, "Between the humble and contrite heart and the majesty of heaven there are no barriers; the only password is prayer." It bothers me that so few people seem to use that "password" and thereby deny unto themselves so many of the blessings of heaven which are available to them.

"The humble and contrite heart" is the first essential. One of the finest verses in the Bible is 2 Chronicles 7:14: "If my people, which are called by my name, shall humble themselves, and pray. . . ." Notice that we are not told to pray for humility; we are told to humble ourselves. It is such a temptation to become proud, to feel self-sufficient, to recognize no need for God. Sometimes we must be put on our backs before we ever look up.

Too many of us are like the Pharisee in the temple who prayed, "I thank thee, that I am not as other men are . . ." (Luke 18:11). We compare ourselves with someone who has failed along the way and we take secret pride in another's downfall. That is the reason we are so attracted to gossip—it makes us look so good in comparison! Not enough of us are like the publican who prayed, "God be merciful to me a sinner" (Luke 18:13).

Not only must one be humble in order to pray, he must also have faith. There is probably no passage in the Bible which I read more often than Mark 11:22–26; that is the passage which describes how faith can remove mountains, and in which Jesus said, "I say unto you, What things soever ye desire, when ye pray, believe that ye receive them, and ye shall have them."

Believing is a process of mental picturing. So often, instead of picturing the answer we want, we continue to look at the troubles we have. We concentrate on our fears instead of our faith, our problems instead of our powers, our sins instead of our Saviour.

In that same passage, after He had talked about faith and believing, Jesus said something else: "And when ye stand praying, forgive, if ye have aught against any. . . ." A wrong spirit toward another person, hate, hurt feelings, envy, jealousy, can block out your prayers completely.

Humility and faith are two essentials of effective prayer. The third essential you will find in John 15:7: "If ye abide in me, and my words abide in you, ye shall ask what ye will, and it shall be done unto you." The key word is *abide*. Sometimes the answer comes immediately, sometimes the answer tarries—but we must continue close to Christ, developing our love for Him, allowing His love to fill our own lives more completely, meditating day and night upon His words.

Jesus said, ". . . men ought always to pray, and not to faint" (Luke 18:1). "To faint" means "to give up, to quit." Many times we miss the answer because we stop praying too soon. Humility, faith, abide—those are the three key words to answered prayer.

## A-C-T-S-S

It is easy to get into a spiritual rut and reach the place where we go through the motions without receiving the power. This is especially true in our praying. It is a temptation to say the same words every time we pray without really thinking and without putting our hearts into what we are saying. I am constantly seeking to develop new spiritual techniques. Recently I have hit upon an acronym that I like to keep in mind when I pray. The word is ACTSS (*acts* with an extra s). It is an appropriate word for prayer because all prayer should result in acts.

A is for adoration. Surely all prayer should begin with our thinking of the Lord. The most wonderful collection of prayers is the Book of Psalms. Sometime read some of the psalms, and notice how much of them is given to praising God: "O Lord our Lord, how excellent is thy name in all the earth!" (8:1); "I will sing unto the Lord, because he hath dealt bountifully with me" (13:6).

Kahlil Gibran, in *The Prophet*, says, "You pray in your distress and in your need; would that you might pray also in the fullness of your joy and in the days of abundance." All real prayer begins in adoration of God.

C is for confession. As one feels the presence of God, as one thinks of His purity and righteousness, he naturally feels even as Isaiah felt. When Isaiah saw the Lord high and lifted up, he fell on his face, saying,"I am undone; because I am a man of unclean lips . . ." (6:5). We read in 1 John 1:9, "If we confess our sins, he is faithful and just to forgive us our sins, and to cleanse us from all unrighteousness." That is a wonderful promise.

T is for thanksgiving. One of my favorite songs is "Count your many blessings, name them one by one." Many people never think of God except when they want something. Like any father, God is glad when His children come asking; but don't you suppose He also wants us to talk with Him sometimes about the things that He has already given?

S is for supplication; that is, prayer for others. In 1 Samuel 12:23, we read, "God forbid that I should sin against the Lord in ceasing to pray for you. . . ." Also notice the wording in the Lord's Prayer: the pronouns "our" and "us" predominate. Never forget that praying for another person makes a difference to that person.

The last S is for submission. "Not my will, but thine, be done" (Luke 22:42). Prayer is not a means by which I seek to control God; it is a means of putting myself in a position where God can control me. Instead of my prayer being "Give me," it must become "Take me."

## Persistence in Prayer

Ask, and it shall be given you; seek, and ye shall find; knock, and it shall be opened unto you:

For every one that asketh receiveth; and he that seeketh
  findeth; and to him that knocketh it shall be opened.
Or what man is there of you, whom if his son ask bread,
  will he give him a stone?
Or if he ask a fish, will he give him a serpent?
If ye then, being evil, know how to give good gifts unto
  your children, how much more shall your Father
  which is in heaven give good things to them that ask
  him? (Matthew 7:7–11).

Many reasons are given as to why people do not pray, such as:
lack of faith, or not knowing how to pray, or the knowledge that
there are things in one's life that make one ashamed to face God.
Seldom are these the real reasons why people fail to pray. The real
reason why many people do not pray is simply that they have
nothing to pray for. The supreme tragedy of many people's lives is
that they want so little and are satisfied with almost nothing. They
have no high dreams nor lofty hopes, no great ambitions nor
burning desires. Wanting nothing, they pray for nothing. Too
many people are satisfied with life just as it is.

Someone asked Raphael, "Which is your greatest painting?" He
replied, "My next one." In contrast, consider the attitude of the
president of the Pierce-Arrow automobile company, who, in the
year 1910, said, "We have built the finest car it will ever be possible
to build. No improvements can ever be made." It has been a long
time now since any Pierce-Arrow car has been made.

Let some great need come into the life of any person, and he will
naturally pray. To one who has need of prayer Jesus said, "Ask
. . . seek . . . knock." In the original Greek, these three words are
used in the present tense, and they call for continuing action. The
better translation is: "Keep on asking . . . keep on seeking . . .
keep on knocking."

The first step in prayer is to *ask*. This means three things:

1. To ask implies a sense of need and an admission of
   helplessness. The blind man on the corner asks for help.
   He is merely begging because he offers nothing in return,
   and when we pray before God there are times when we
   can only come asking. However, we are His children, and
   a child has the right to ask his Father without shame.
2. To ask means to apply to a person. A tree is beautiful, but

one cannot ask a tree for anything because a tree cannot respond. To pray means that one must be conscious that there is a personal God who hears.

3. To ask is to be definite. The Apostle Paul said, "Let your requests be made known unto God" (Philippians 4:6).

The second step in prayer is to *seek*. Seeking means asking plus effort. When Jesus told us to pray, "Give us this day our daily bread," He did not mean that we are to expect God simply to rain down manna from heaven. Rather, this means "Give us the opportunity to earn our bread." For the farmer, it means the opportunity to plow the field, and plant the seeds, and cultivate the crops. For others, it means the opportunity to use the money they have earned as a result of their labors to buy the bread. The prayer "Thy Kingdom come" means that we commit ourselves to the task of building it. Seeking means using what we have to answer our own prayers, expecting God to add to our resources.

The third step in prayer is to *knock*. Knocking is asking plus effort plus persistence. Jesus told the story of a man who continued to knock on his neighbor's door at midnight until the man inside got up and answered his request. Moffatt's translation has it: "I tell you, though he will not get up and give you anything because you are a friend of his, he will at least rise and give you whatever you want because you persist" (Luke 11:5–8 MOFFATT).

In another place Jesus said that "men ought always to pray, and not to faint" (Luke 18:1). To faint means to quit. One may allow bitterness or disappointment or lack of understanding or hopelessness to turn him away from God. How long must one keep on praying? Until the answer comes. Earlier in the Sermon on the Mount, Jesus said, "Your Father knoweth what things ye have need of, before ye ask him" (Matthew 6:8). But it is often true that we ourselves do not know what we need, and God mercifully withholds His answer until we come with the right request. God may say no to our request, but that is no reason for us to stop praying. Remember, *no* is not God's final answer. We must continue to pray until we get God's *yes*. So, Jesus points out, just as a father would not give his son a stone when he asked for bread, the heavenly Father will give His children "good things to them that ask him."

We remember that when Augustine was a youth, he wanted to go to Rome. Rome was a wild and wicked city, and his mother,

Monica, prayed persistently that her son would be prevented from going there. However, one day she stood on the shore and saw a ship sailing away, bearing her son to Rome. She might have felt that God had refused to hear and answer her prayer. However, she did not stop praying for her boy. In Rome, Augustine heard a great sermon and was converted and became one of the saints of the church. Suppose Monica had stopped praying when she received the answer *no*. Her real prayer was not that her son might be prevented from going to Rome. Rather it was that her son might become the Christian that he did become. Her real prayer was answered with a *yes*, but along the pathway of her prayer she received some answers which were *no*. We are never to stop praying until we get the *yes* answer.

## The Nine Prayer Steps

To make the most of prayer, let me suggest nine prayer steps. There are three steps to take *before* prayer:

1. Decide what you really want. Have clearly in mind exactly what you plan to ask in prayer.
2. Determine whether or not what you want is right. Ask yourself questions such as: "Is it fair to everyone else concerned?" "Is it best for me?" "Is it in harmony with the Spirit of God?"
3. Write it down. Reducing your requests to writing helps to clarify your thinking and deepen the impressions upon your mind and heart.

Then there are three steps to take *during* prayer:

4. Keep your mind still. Just as the moon cannot be perfectly reflected on a restless sea, God cannot be experienced by an unquiet mind. "Be still, and know that I am God" (Psalms 46:10). At this point we must concentrate to keep the mind from wandering. There are some books I cannot read while in a comfortable chair, and there are some prayers I cannot pray without being completely at attention. This is what Jesus meant when He said, "When thou hast shut thy door . . ." (Matthew 6:6); that is, shut out distracting thoughts.

5. Talk with God, and not to God. Instead of saying with Samuel, "Speak; for thy servant heareth" (1 Samuel 3:10), we are prone to say, "Listen, Lord, for Thy servant speaketh." Prayer is both speaking and listening.
6. Promise God what you yourself will do to answer your own prayer. God answers prayer, not for you, but with you. Jesus performed many of His miracles by giving the person to be helped something to do. As you pray, search for the things that you can do yourself.

Then, there are three steps to take *after* prayer:

7. Always remember to thank God for answering your prayer. You would not pray in the first place if you did not believe God would answer. Now, confirm that belief by thanking Him for the answer, even though it has not yet come.
8. Be willing to accept whatever God's answer may be, remembering the words of our Lord, "Nevertheless, not my will, but thine, be done" (Luke 22:42).
9. Do everything loving that comes to your mind. One of the objects of prayer is to bring the love of God into our hearts; and as we express that love, we make it possible for God to answer our prayers.

## Intercession

Does it help for one person to pray for another? Since prayer for another does make a difference, the Bible tells us it is a sin not to pray for others: "God forbid that I should sin against the Lord in ceasing to pray for you" (1 Samuel 12:23). I believe intercession helps in at least four ways.

1. Prayer helps by helping the person who prays. A man spoke to me about someone who had done him great wrong. "Don't preach to me about forgiveness. I am not interested in that," he said. I replied, "I only ask you to do one thing—call that man's name in your prayers." Just that act, if sustained, will put out the hot emotional fires in your soul and allow you to think with reason. Prayer will act as a boomerang and be a powerful influence upon the person who sends it out.

2. Prayer has a psychological effect on the person being prayed

for. When the great Martin Luther felt particularly strong and happy, he would exclaim, "I feel as if I were being prayed for." Once, during a difficult time in England's history, Oliver Cromwell wrote his admirals at sea: "You have a plentiful stock of prayers going up for you daily, which is to us and I trust will be to you a matter of great encouragement." Every so often someone writes me just to tell me that he or she is praying for me. Such a letter in the morning makes my entire day different. I have learned to accept criticism without undue concern or bother, but I never want to learn to accept the fact of someone speaking to God on my behalf without joy and inspiration. If you are praying for someone in need, let that one know you are praying for him or her.

3. Praying for another person inspires the one praying to constructive action. There is an old story of a group of church people visiting a poor family to pray with them. They found they needed food and clothing, so together they all knelt and began to pray. After a time, one man's heart was stirred to the point that he reached into his pocket and pulled out some money and put it on the table. The others followed his example and by the time they left, they had answered their own prayers. That is a simple illustration, but there is hardly a person who uses all his own resources. Prayer clears our vision and helps us to see better what can be done; prayer gives us inspiration to get up and start doing what we can.

4. Most important, prayer brings the power of God to bear upon a person or situation. The Bible says, "The prayer of faith shall save the sick" (James 5:15). It isn't the faith of the one being prayed for, but rather the faith of the one praying that makes the difference. If I have faith and pray for another, whether or not the other person has faith, my prayers will be effective.

Picture a person in one room of a house. Think of God being in the next room. Between the two is a wall. If you stand in the doorway, you can be in contact with the one in each room. One could speak to the other through you. Between many people and God there are walls—unbelief, unconcern, and wrongdoing, to name a few. But if you have contact with both God and that person, you become the connection between the two. That is what intercessory prayer is all about.

Don't commit the sin of failing to pray for others. This is one of the most important of all Christian duties.

# 5

# *The Fifth Spiritual Wonder:*

# The Power of Faith

Today we have planes that travel faster than the speed of sound. The principle of that plane existed in Abraham's day, but he did not know how to develop it. Thus, he did well to travel a mere four miles per hour. Instead of sailing through the sky, he traveled by foot or in a slow wagon. We might pity poor Abraham. Once he had to take a journey. It was not an easy one and lesser men would have shrunk from it. He did not know what the end would be or what he would meet along the way. Though he did not possess the marvelous power we today have learned to use, he did possess a power even better. The Bible says, "By faith Abraham . . . went out, not knowing whither he went" (Hebrews 11:8).

In our desire for physical power, many of us have lost inner spiritual power. Remember, the same God who created a power that can light up a room also created a power that can light up a life. The God who created a power that can pull a train across a mountain also created a power that can pull a person across the steep and hard places of life.

Faith may be divided into three categories, each of which can lead to the others:

1. There is the faith of nature. Archibald Rutledge tells of seeing a bird build its nest. Patiently and hard it worked all day. That night a storm came and the next morning the little bird's home lay on the ground in pathetic ruin. But the bird was there, too. It was

not mourning over the destruction, instead it was busily rebuilding.

That is the faith of nature. It does not ask why. Instead it picks
up and goes on, no matter what happens. I saw a stump from
which a big tree had been cut. Out of the stump was growing a tiny
sapling which some day would take the old tree's place. Tragedies
come but nature faith immediately sets about the task of rebuilding.

2. There is human faith, which goes a step farther than nature
faith. Human faith grows out of the basic conviction that life is good
and can be trusted. It says with hymnist Washington Gladden:

> *I know that right is right;*
> *That it is not good to lie;*
> *That love is better than spite,*
> *And a neighbor than a spy. . . .*
>
> *In the darkest night of the year,*
> *When the stars have all gone out,*
> *That courage is better than fear,*
> *That faith is truer than doubt.*

Human faith maintains the integrity of the soul. No matter what
happens, human faith leads us to know that it is always better to
be good than bad, to be brave than a coward, that honor and
integrity must never be sacrificed.

3. There is our faith in God. Some years ago I wanted to raise
some money to remodel a little country church of which I was
pastor. I called a meeting of the members one Saturday night. To
my bitter disappointment, only a very few of the people came. At
first I thought I would call off the meeting. Then I decided I would
talk to the few who came about the program, but would not take
the collection. I knew I could not expect much from so few.

I mentioned my decision about not bothering to take a collection
to a godly old man who was there. He looked at me with contempt
and said, "I am ashamed of you. You have no business being
pastor of any church." He told me I was trying to do God's work
and that I should never back up. "Go ahead," he said, "make your
plea, take the offering, and have faith in God." I did what he said
and that night we got $37.00 more than we needed.

Faith in God means that you believe that if you do your best,

God will see you through. As William Carey expressed it, "Attempt great things for God. Expect big things of God."

May we go out *by faith*.

## Faith Steps

"How can I get faith?" is a question frequently asked. For an answer let's look at a man who had faith and see how he got it. This man had such a wonderful faith that even Jesus marveled at it. The Lord said, "I have not found so great faith, no, not in Israel." The man was a centurion, a soldier. His parents were heathen so probably he had no childhood training in the faith. His faith was one he acquired in later life. As you read the account of this man in Luke 7:1–10, you will find four ways he attained his faith.

1. He found something definite in which to believe. In his case it was a man by the name of Jesus. Rumors of the preacher from the little town of Nazareth had come to him. He might have dismissed those rumors as did some others by saying, "There is nothing to that man. He is just creating a little emotional excitement and soon he will be forgotten."

Instead, he studied the man. He listened to what others said about Jesus. He doubtless went to hear Him preach, he watched His miracles, he observed His way of living. On the basis of the evidence, he decided that Jesus was beyond the ordinary, that Jesus was more than a mere man. Thus, when he had a need in his own household, because Jesus had wrought wonders in others, it was not hard for the centurion to believe Jesus could do the same for him.

We can take this step by reading the Gospels—Matthew, Mark, Luke, and John. Read Mark first. It does not take long to read those sixteen short chapters. Read it just as you would any other story. Don't worry about the meaning of every verse—just read the story, see what He did, what He said, how He lived. First, think of Him as a man who once lived. Before you can believe in Christ the Son of God, you must get acquainted with Jesus the Man of Galilee. As you learn about Him, it comes easily and naturally to have faith in Him.

2. Another thing the centurion did was to support the church. The account says he built a church. Now I know the church is not all that it ought to be. There are many hypocrites in the church;

ministers often preach dull sermons; the church does not do what it can and should do.

I have noticed this, however: people who recognize the faults of the church but support it with their prayers, attendance, gifts, and service to make the church what it ought to be, find that it does a lot for them. Faith is like a boomerang: begin using what you have and it comes back to you in greater measure. I have never met one person of genuine faith who was not active in some church.

3. This centurion attained faith because of his humility. He said to Christ, "I am not worthy that thou shouldest enter under my roof." Pride and a haughty spirit always kill faith. A conceited person never really finds God because he feels no need for God. As long as we are sufficient unto ourselves, God cannot come into our lives. I frequently say one can pray anywhere, anytime—walking down the street, washing the dishes, or doing anything. But I can pray nowhere as effectively as on my knees. The position of the body has an influence on the soul. The very act of kneeling is an expression of humility.

4. Finally, this centurion was led to faith by having faith in his fellow men. Being a member of another race, wearing the uniform of the despised Roman army, it was natural for the Jews to hate him. Instead, they loved him and sought to help him. I am sure their attitude was first brought about by his attitude toward them. Though he was hated, he refused to hate back. He saw something good in them and they in turn saw good in him. People are made in the image of God and as we practice believing in God's image, it becomes easier to believe in God.

## You Have to Have Faith

I have never known faith to be described better than by G. A. Studdert-Kennedy. His poem-essay entitled "Faith" is one that I have read again and again through the years. I would like to share it with you:

> How do I know that God is good? I don't.
> I gamble like a man. I bet my life
> Upon one side in life's great war. I must,
> I can't stand out. I must take sides. The man
> Who is a neutral in this fight is not
> A man. He's bulk and body without breath,

Cold leg of lamb without mint sauce. A fool.
He makes me sick. Good Lord! Weak tea!
    Cold slops!
I want to live, live out, not wobble through
My life somehow, and then into the dark.
I must have God. This life's too dull without,
Too dull for aught but suicide. What's man
To live for else? I'd murder someone just
To see red blood. I'd drink myself blind drunk
And see blue snakes if I could not look up
To see blue skies, and hear God speaking through
The silence of the stars. How is it proved?
It isn't proved, you fool, it can't be proved.
How can you prove a victory before
It's won? How can you prove a man who leads,
To be a leader worth the following.
Unless you follow to the death—and out
Beyond mere death, which is not anything
But Satan's lie upon eternal life?
Well—God's my leader, and I hold that He
        is good, and strong enough to work His plan
And purpose out to its appointed end.
I am no fool, I have my reasons for
This faith, but they are not the reasonings,
The coldly calculated formula
Of thought divorced from feeling. They are true,
Too true for that. There's no such thing as thought
Which does not feel, if it be real thought.
And not thought's ghost—all pale and sicklied o'er
With dead conventions—abstract truths—man's lie
Upon this living, loving, suff'ring Truth,
That pleads and pulses in my very veins,
The blue blood of all beauty, and the breath
        of life itself. I see what God has done,
What life in this world is. I see what you
See, this eternal struggle in the dark.
I see the foul disorders, and the filth
Of mind and soul, in which men, wallowing
Like swine, stomp on their brothers till they drown
In puddles of stale blood, and vomitings
Of their corruption. This life stinks in places,

*'Tis true, yet scent of roses and of hay*
*New mown comes stealing on the evening breeze,*
    *and through the market's din, the bargaining*
    *of cheats, who make God's world a den of*
    *thieves.*
*I hear sweet bells ring out to prayer, and see*
*The faithful kneeling by the Calvary of Christ.*
    *I walk in crowded streets where men*
*And women, mad with lust, loose-lipped and lewd,*
*Go promenading down to hell's wide gates;*
*Yet have I looked into my mother's eyes,*
*And seen the light that never was on sea*
*Or land, the light of Love, pure Love and true,*
*And on that Love I bet my life. I back*
*My mother 'gainst a whore when I believe*
*In God, and can a man do less or more?*
*I have to choose. I back the scent of life*
*Against its stink. That's what Faith works out at*
*Finally. I know not why the Evil,*
*I know not why the Good, both mysteries*
*Remain unsolved, and both insoluble.*
*I know that both are there, the battle set,*
*And I must fight on this side or on that.*
*I can't stand shiv'ring on the bank, I plunge*
*Head first. I bet my life on Beauty, Truth,*
*And Love, not abstract but incarnate Truth,*
*Not Beauty's passing shadow but its Self.*
*Its very Self made flesh, Love realized.*
*I bet my life on Christ—Christ Crucified.*

## Doubts About God

As we discuss faith, we come to the question of our belief in God. There is a verse which I have often read and most of us have experienced in some moment of life: "The Lord said that he would dwell in the thick darkness" (1 Kings 8:12). I am reminded of how the great Harry Emerson Fosdick once began a sermon in the Riverside Church in New York. He said:

Once more today I feel what I commonly feel when I face worshipping congregations. You look so pious. You are so reverent. You listen so respectfully to Scripture and anthem. You sing so earnestly the resounding hymns. But I know and you know that in every life there is something else which our worship does not express—doubts, questions, incertainties, skepticism. Every one of us, facing the Christian faith, must honestly say what the man in the gospel story said to Jesus. "Lord, I believe; help thou mine unbelief" (Mark 9:24).

## Four Thoughts About God

In reference to our doubts about God, let me make several observations. First, doubt is not a sin. If you read the autobiographies of even the greatest saints, you will find them expressing doubts from time to time. Christ did not condemn Thomas for his doubts.

A second fact about God is that He seems so far away. As children we grew up with the idea that God was way up yonder somewhere.

In the third place, we deal with the silence of God. As Jesus was hanging on the Cross, God did not say a word and He was moved to cry out, "My God, my God, why hast thou forsaken me?" (Matthew 27:46). And in the midst of our crosses we do not hear God's voice and our faith is shaken.

A fourth problem we have is that we have no vocabulary with which we can adequately talk about God. With our very limited knowledge, there is no way that we can intelligently discuss an infinite God. This leaves us frustrated and confused.

## Having the Power of Faith

Increasingly through the years I have believed that no person is ever defeated until he or she thinks he is. We have tremendous powers if we use them. One of the ministers in my early years whom I loved and gained a lot from was Dean Ramundo de Ovies. He was dean of the Episcopal Cathedral in Atlanta, Georgia, for many years. I had the privilege of being with him on a number of occasions and he always inspired me. He was a great storyteller and I shall never forget one story that he told me. I have heard this story credited to other sources, but nobody ever told it better than Dean de Ovies.

When he was a boy he lived in England. He explained that they had a habit of catching sparrows in the cemeteries at night. The next day their mother would make sparrow pie and it was delicious. He explained to me that it would usually take about twenty sparrows to make a pie. These sparrows would roost in the vines of the cemetery and while they were asleep, they were easily caught.

One night he was in the cemetery catching sparrows and he fell into a newly dug grave. The grave was so deep that he could not get out. He tried every way he knew but would fail. Finally, in exhaustion, he sat down in a corner to wait until morning. Presently he heard the footsteps of another boy who had come into the graveyard looking for sparrows. The boy was whistling—as people are apt to do in graveyards at night. He recognized him as his friend, Charlie. His first thought was to call out to Charlie and ask his help, but he decided to wait for a while and see what happened. Sure enough, Charlie slipped into the same grave. Dean de Ovies explained that he sat quietly in the corner as Charlie tried to get out. But, he could not climb over the side, either. After a while, Dean de Ovies said in a deep voice, "Can't you let a man enjoy his own grave in peace?"

The result was electric. Charlie got out over the side of that grave as if he had wings. He thought he could not get out of that grave, but he discovered that he could! I believe we all have unused powers with which, if properly motivated, we can accomplish things we never dreamed we could accomplish.

In my book *Prayer Changes Things*, I discussed the power of faith and described five laws of faith:

1. You always have faith. Every so often somebody will ask the question, "How can I find faith?" Or I hear people say, "I have lost my faith." Life has a way of smothering our faith. Loved ones can die, businesses can fail, jobs can be lost, friends can betray, lives can be ruined. Wrecks and fires and earthquakes and wars and all the troubles of life can come in upon us. They have a tendency to fill our minds and overwhelm us. But the truth is, no person ever loses faith.

I love the old Chinese tale of the fish who overheard the fisherman say, "Have you ever stopped to think how essential water is? Without water the world would dry up and all life would die."

The little fish in the lake, when they heard that, became

panic-stricken. They began saying to each other, "We must hurriedly find water at once." They asked the other fish in the lake where to find water, but no one seemed to know. Finally, they swam out into the river, but the fish in the river could not tell them where to find water. They replied, "You are in water right now—you have never left it." So it is with our faith. We are born with it; we never really lose it.

2. Always start with your faith instead of your fears. I knew a lady who was paralyzed in one leg. She spent all of her time in a wheelchair. Her doctor said to her that she ought to get up and walk. But she protested that, because of her paralyzed leg, she could not possibly walk. The doctor had her stand up and then told her to walk. She put forth this paralyzed leg and as she moved her weight on to it she immediately began to fall. He caught her. Then he said to her, "Remember, you can always walk if you will step out on your good leg first."

3. No matter what happens, hold on to your faith. In Vienna, Austria, it has long been sport to swim down the Danube River. But in the river there are whirlpools and sometimes a swimmer will get caught in a whirlpool and will drown. Wise swimmers know that when one is caught in a whirlpool, if he will just be still, the whirlpool will push the swimmer back to the surface and to safety.

In the stream of life we get caught in troubles and sometimes we get panicky, but if we will just keep our cool, gradually we will rise above this problem.

4. Do not be afraid to trust your heart. It was Pascal who said, "The heart has its reasons which reason knows nothing of." Faith is never unreasonable, but sometimes we have deep impulses that we cannot explain. Sometimes our feelings are stronger than our reasons, and many times we ought to obey our deep feelings.

5. Maintain a spirit of humility. A story that has always made a profound impression on me is about a college girl who visited the home of Beethoven. She slipped under the rope and began playing Beethoven's piano. She said to the one in charge, "I suppose every musician who comes here wants to play this piano?" He explained to her that recently the great Paderewski was visiting there and someone asked him to play that piano. He replied, "No, I do not feel worthy to play the great master's piano."

I know that at times I have been accused of being less than humble—perhaps at times justly so—but really I do not think so. I have spent my life in places and in positions that I did not feel worthy of. The first time I ever stood up to preach, I did not feel worthy to stand in the pulpit, and I was very uncomfortable. Really, that has been my experience through the years. I have always felt a genuine inadequacy for every job that I have had. Especially have I felt misjudged by my preacher friends. If they knew the actual truth, I believe they would say, "Charles knows the meaning of humility." I think many, many times of that night in Gethsemane when the disciples did not feel the need to pray. I have always felt that need.

## Learn to Have Faith

Learn to have faith. The first cause of failure is lack of faith. Failure and faith are incompatible words—they simply cannot exist together. If you have faith, you will not fail; if you fail, it is a sign that you do not have faith. Faith may have setbacks, but faith never knows failure.

The famous football coach Knute Rockne had four rules for the selection of the boys on his great Notre Dame teams. He said: (1) I will not have a boy with a swelled head, for you cannot teach him anything; (2) I will not have a griper, kicker, or complainer; (3) I will allow no dissipation; (4) I will not have a boy with an inferiority complex—he must believe he can accomplish things.

Read again Rockne's fourth rule; it is the most important. The psychologist William James, who probably understood people better than any American who has ever lived, confirmed Mr. Rockne's rule. He said, "Our belief at the beginning of a doubtful undertaking is the one thing that assures the successful outcome of our ventures." Note that he said "the *one* thing."

But faith is not something that suddenly comes to a person in some magical manner; it is something that must be learned. The best guide I know for learning faith is contained in these words from the Bible: "Jesus said unto him, If thou canst believe, all things are possible to him that believeth. And straightway the father of the child cried out, and said with tears, Lord, I believe . . ." (Mark 9:23, 24).

The first step is to get the word "impossible" out of our vocabulary. We begin losing faith by saying, "It can't be done," or something similar. We begin learning faith by believing it can be done.

Here is a little plan that works wonders: keep count of the times in one day when you say or think something is impossible; at the end of the day write that number down. The next day concentrate on reducing the times you allow yourself to think in a negative fashion. See how many times you reduced the number of the previous day. Continue day by day to reduce your use of "impossible," and gradually you will see more and more areas of your life move into the realm of the possible. You will develop new courage and strength as faith begins to grow within you.

But that is not the full answer. Notice, the man replied, "Lord, I believe." Merely to say "I believe" tremendously increases one's power, but to begin with "Lord" is far greater. In fact, true faith must begin with God. We recall that Jesus said, "The things which are impossible with men are possible with God" (Luke 18:27).

The longer I live, the less confidence I have in myself, but the more confidence I have in God. I am conscious of my own weaknesses and limitations, but I have become increasingly conscious of God's strength and power. And as I shift my confidence from myself to God, I find my faith becoming stronger. I don't always see how, but I know that somehow God will always know what to do and will have the power to do it. That gives me faith.

## Get Rid of Your Spirit of Infirmity

It is pathetic to see so many people stumbling through life half-defeated, unhappy, frustrated, and often bitter and disappointed. Life can be a wonderful experience.

One of the finest stories in the Bible is only three verses long—Luke 13:11–13. There was a woman whose back was so bent she was "bowed together." That is a terrible handicap. Jesus saw her—He always has an eye out for those who need help. The Bible says, "He called her to him. . . ." He is the same Christ today as He was then. At this very moment He may be concerned with your need. He may be calling in some way to you.

Remember that Luke recorded this story. Luke was a medical doctor. He had treated many people and had become a wise student of human nature. He saw that the woman's trouble was not really her bent back; he reported that she had "a spirit of infirmity." For eighteen years her back had been bent. But the bent back had got into her mind, leaving her with a sense of handicap, inferiority, defeat.

To her Jesus said, "Woman, thou art loosed from thine infirmity." In that instance He did straighten her back; but that was not the important thing. He took the bent back out of her mind and enabled her to face up to life with confidence, whether or not her back was bent. He enabled her to rise above that which was defeating her. She found new joy and peace in life.

## Understand and Accept Yourself

That experience can come to any one of us. When something is defeating us, we can gain power over it and find new confidence by doing three things. First, we must be willing to understand and accept ourselves. The great psychologist William James quoted a woman as saying, "The happiest day in my life was the day I admitted the fact that I am not physically beautiful and stopped worrying about it."

All my life I have been underweight. People would talk about how thin I was and it worried me. I did everything I heard about to gain weight. I worried about getting sick. Then one glad day a sensible physician said to me, "You were born skinny and will be all your life, so stop trying to do anything about it." I accepted his advice and have followed it ever since. I am still skinny but the fact is out of my mind; it is not a problem to me any longer.

In the play *Green Pastures,* Noah said, "I ain't much, but I'se all I got." When one accepts that fact, life takes on new meaning and power. I think of Evelyn Harrala who was born without either hands or feet. She decided one day that since nothing could be done about her handicaps, she would do all she could in spite of them. She graduated from college with honors, became an accomplished organist, and was a valuable member on the staff of a large church.

General William Booth, founder of the Salvation Army and one of the great men of all time, was informed that he was going blind. He said, "I have done what I could for God with two eyes. Now I will do what I can without any eyes."

All of us have handicaps of one sort or another. We can let the handicap get into our minds and defeat us, or we can go on in spite of ourselves and win victories.

## You Are Not Alone

There is a second step to gaining assurance. Someone quotes the prayer of a humble old man: "Lord, help me to understand that

You are going to let nothing happen that You and I can't handle together." If I thought I had to do by myself the things I have planned for the next twelve months, with only my own strength and resources, I would give up and quit this minute.

One of the reasons people lose confidence and get shaky is that they realize they do not have the abilities and strength to do the things they feel they must do. But I don't depend only on myself; I know that other people will help me. Also, I know the Lord will help me.

The last time I talked with Dr. Norman Vincent Peale, we talked about our wives and what blessings they are. During the worst part of the Depression, his church in New York was having difficulty meeting its budget. One day his wife said to him, "Our church ought to take over the full support of another missionary." He did not see how they could add $1200 to their budget at that time, and that was the amount required. He turned her down.

But some wives—most wives—are hard to turn down. She said, "You might as well go ahead and do it because I am going to pray about it." A few weeks later a man attended that church, made a decision for Christ, and joined. A few mornings later Dr. Peale was opening his mail and there was a letter from that man, enclosing a pledge card and a check for $1200! Dr. Peale thinks the Lord answered his wife's prayer, and I think so, too.

Of course, God answers different prayers in different ways, but God always does answer. I was talking with one of the best-known newspaper writers in this country. We were talking about prayer and he told me that the two things he had prayed hardest for, he had lost. He had fervently asked God to save the life of his baby boy who was sick, but the little fellow died. Later he and his wife had another son, but he was born with the life flickering in him. This man walked the corridors of the hospital praying, but they never got the baby home alive.

Yet, he is not bitter; neither did he lose his faith. He told me that often, as he is walking along the street, he feels the need of prayer and stops right where he is and talks to the Lord. And he spoke of several instances when almost miraculous answers to prayers have come. He doesn't ask why he lost those two little boys; he trusts God and he goes on.

I have constantly said to my own children, "When you need help in any way, always let me know." I would be very disappointed if one of them said, "I won't ever need you again. I'll handle everything by myself." I want to take a part in their lives. And our heavenly Father feels that way about each of us.

## The Faith You Keep Will Keep You

Thomas à Kempis expressed one of the fundamental principles of victorious living when he said, "If thou bear the cross, it will soon bear thee." That has been proven again and again. Some time ago, I was in the office of a very successful businessman. It is an elegant office with expensive furnishings, big leather chairs, air-conditioning, and every detail just right. This man has a big business; he is wealthy and highly respected. He has undertaken daring enterprises and has come out on top.

I said, "Tell me the secret of your life." He hesitated for a few moments; he seemed to be lost in some very sacred memory. Then slowly he began to talk about an older brother who was brilliant and good and was great even at the age of twenty-eight when he died. This man was a boy of only fourteen when his brother got sick. The family was too poor to afford a nurse, and it fell to his lot to nurse his brother.

His brother was sick for months, and there were many unpleasant tasks to perform. In the latter stages of his brother's illness, there were times he could hardly bear to do what needed to be done. But he loved his brother, and he carried out those distasteful tasks without complaint. "Always," he said, "when I had done what I could and the task was finished, I felt good about it. After my brother died, I forgot about the unpleasant part of nursing him and I thought about how glad I was I had done it."

Later on this boy grew to manhood, but life did not come easy for him. There were a lot of hard jobs to be done, a lot of times when he wanted to give up and quit. But day by day, he did his best at the job before him. And then, when he went to bed at night, he felt good inside. He knew he had done what he should have. He learned and practiced one of life's greatest truths: the cross bears those who bear the cross.

Leaving his office, I began thinking of how Paul expressed it. He simply said "I have kept the faith" (2 Timothy 4:7). Those words come near the end of what probably was the last letter the Apostle ever wrote. Soon afterward he was led from his prison cell and executed. He was writing to his young friend, Timothy, telling him to stand firm always, hold true to the course, endure the afflictions.

As an old man, Paul could look back and see many times when he was tempted to give up, but day by day, through each hard experience, he "kept the faith." Now at the end of the way, he pointed out, "Demas hath forsaken me . . . Alexander the coppersmith did me much evil . . . No man stood with me." But in spite of everything, he was serene and not afraid.

He said, "Notwithstanding the Lord stood with me . . ." (2 Timothy 4:17). At the end of the way, when the going is the roughest, we see that the faith he kept, kept him.

A very wise man who had spent his life dealing with people once said to me, "Every person who ever attained greatness had to fight the temptation of committing suicide." Maybe for most of us the temptation has not been that extreme, but certainly time after time we are tempted to give up and quit. In fact, most of us have at times given up. Not many can look back over all the experiences of life and say with Paul, "I have kept the faith."

There have been times when we have not been our best. Of those times we are ashamed. But, thank God, we can also look back upon times when we did "keep the faith." Of those times we are very proud. The victories we have won are now our strongest supports. The faith we kept is keeping us—the crosses we bore are now bearing us.

Max Beerbohm wrote a story called "The Happy Hypocrite." It is about Lord George Hell, who was an unscrupulous villain. Not only was he mean inside, he looked the part outside. Just seeing his face made people afraid of him. He fell in love with a young girl, Little Miss Mere, who was both beautiful and innocent. She refused him, however, because as she said, "I can never be the wife of a man whose face is not saintly."

Because he wanted her so much, Lord George Hell had the finest maskmaker make him a mask that was saintly. With the mask of a saint, he again sought the love of Miss Mere and won it, and they were married. Day by day he sought to keep up his hypocrisy. He was careful to be unselfish, attentive, and patient. He constantly held in check his evil tendencies in order to appear a saint.

But one day an old enemy found him, and in the presence of his lovely wife, ruthlessly tore off Lord Hell's mask. But when the mask was removed, a saint's face was revealed. He had actually become what he had practiced being day by day. The faith that he had kept in the end had kept him. Practice keeping faith day by day, and one day you will have enough to keep you.

## Look Back and Remember

There are three thoughts to keep in mind which will help us to keep our faith. The first is: when tempted to give up or lose faith, look back and remember the times you won the victory. Maybe it was some crisis fifteen years ago. You did not see how you could go on, but you did go on and it worked out all right. You discovered new courage and strength inside you that you did not know you had.

Later some other crisis came into your life. You did not see a chance for yourself, but you kept holding on. Maybe some friend helped you that you had not counted on. At any rate, you got through it. Some time later, still another crisis developed. You can't explain it, but as you kept walking through the dark, suddenly you came out into the sunshine. It seemed to work out providentially. As you look back now, you decide it was providential.

We do have unused inner resources; there are friends who help; God does take a hand in our lives. And somehow we eventually come to believe that no matter what life does to us, we can go on. That belief helps us to keep the faith.

## Forces That Uphold Us

A second help in keeping the faith is not to forget that, though life has a way of pulling us down, there are even stronger forces in life that hold us up. Life may hurt us, but even more it aids us. Paul said, "I have kept the faith," and in the end, the faith that he kept, kept him. But sometimes it seems almost impossible to keep faith. Remembering the past victories we have won will help us to keep from giving up in some new crisis.

Some years ago, one of the great Sequoia trees in California was cut down. Scientists studied the tree and then told us something of its history. It was a seedling 271 years before Christ was born; 516 years later, it was severely damaged in a forest fire, but nature immediately set to work to repair the damage. Though it was hurt, the tree kept living and growing, and a hundred years later the scar caused by the fire was completely covered. In later years, two other fires damaged the tree, but nature worked to heal those, also.

Life has the power to hurt—to hurt deeply; but life also has the power to heal—to heal completely. When you are tempted to give up your faith, remember that life's helping power is stronger than its hurting power.

## Faith Has Won for Others

A third help for when you are tempted not to keep faith is to consider some of the great triumphs faith has won for others, and to remember that you are made of the same stuff as they were.

Fix in your mind, for example, Mozart. When he was twenty-five, he went to Vienna. There, ten years later, he died. During those ten years he wrote his matchless music, which will live forever. One day his publisher said to him harshly, "Write, sir, in a more easy and popular style; or I will neither print your music nor pay you a penny for it."

Mozart and his wife were so poor that they often had neither food nor fuel in their tiny house. One cold morning that winter, a friend who came to visit Mozart found his house entirely without heat and the composer and his wife waltzing to keep warm. In fact, the cold and hunger put him in his grave when he was thirty-five.

It must have been an almost unbearable temptation for him to sacrifice his standards. He might have so easily said, "After all, a man has to eat." Or even more easily said, "I cannot see my wife suffer." Instead, he said to his publisher, "Then, my good sir, I have only to resign and die of starvation. I cannot write as you demand." And starve he did; but the faith he kept resulted in some of the world's most beautiful music.

And when you are tempted not to keep your faith, it will help you to remember that within you is the same thing that was in Mozart. There is something within every person which, if given a chance, will make that person invincible.

# 6

## *The Sixth Spiritual Wonder:*

# The Gift of Peace

 Once a young man made a list of the things he would like to possess in life. He listed health, love, beauty, talent, power, riches, and fame. He showed his list to a wise man much older in years. After reading the list, the older and wiser man replied: "An excellent list, well digested in content and set down in not-unreasonable order. But it appears, my young friend, that you have omitted the most important element of all. You have forgotten the one ingredient, lacking which, each possession becomes a hideous torment, and your list, as a whole, an intolerable burden."

"And what is that missing ingredient?" the young man asked.

With a pencil the old man crossed out the young man's entire list. Then, underneath he wrote down just three words—peace of mind. The young man was Joshua Liebman who later wrote the book, *Peace of Mind*, which has sold more than a million copies. In fact, there have been many books written on that subject and all of them have had large sales, because more than any other thing— even health, power, or riches—we want peace of mind.

But you do not need to read a book to find the pathway to peace of mind. Jesus summed the entire matter up in just eleven verses— Matthew 6:24–34. Notice the basic principle He sets forth: "No man can serve two masters: for either he will hate the one, and love the other; or else he will hold to the one, and despise the other. Ye cannot serve God and mammon."

The principle is clear—a divided mind is fighting against itself and thus cannot be at peace. Your inner war must be ended by your complete, wholehearted decision. While life demands many decisions, Jesus would have us realize that basically there is just one decision. Settle that one and you settle them all. The decision is: God or mammon. The word *mammon* represents the desires of our body, and *God* represents the longings of our soul. Make up your mind which is more important and give yourself wholly to it. Then you will have peace of mind.

On one occasion Jesus said, "Remember Lot's wife" (Luke 17:32). He might have reminded us of her in connection with this most basic of all decisions, because she is a perfect example of indecision. As a member of a family that gave us our greatest prophets and purest saints, she had within her the faith of her family. She knew God, and from her childhood she had known the meaning of prayer.

But along with her husband she moved into Sodom, the city of mammon. More important, Sodom moved into her. She wanted God, but she also wanted Sodom. Finally the day of final choice came. She made a start toward God, but she looked back toward Sodom. Reaching for the stars with one hand and fingering the mud with the other, she revealed her divided heart, and she ended with misery and eventual destruction.

We must make the choice: "Ye cannot serve God and mammon."

I think the sea is the most complete picture of restlessness I've ever seen. Again and again I have stood upon the seashore and watched the constant movements of the sea. I have never seen it still, not even for one moment. Ceaselessly the ocean tosses itself upon the shores and then runs back again. Why can't the sea lie down and be still? Because it is the victim of a divided mind. The voices of the sky are calling to it. The ocean is drawn upon by the magnets in the heavens. But the muddy old world holds on and demands, "Stay with me." The ocean can never completely decide, and neither can it stop its ears to the voices it hears from the earth and from the heavens. Thus it is always tossing; it never finds rest and peace.

So it is with me and with you. Jesus said, "No man can serve two masters." Until you choose your master, you will never have peace of mind. There are two forces within every person struggling to become the master. One is his ideals, the call of the high life, the desire to be good and godly. The other is his selfish desires, his worldly nature. Goethe said it is regrettable that nature made only one man of him when there is material aplenty for both a rogue and a gentleman. We may choose the low life, but even then we will not have peace because God will never leave us alone. It is as Augustine said, "Man is restless until he finds his rest in Thee, O God."

## Commitment

Consider the picture of our Lord when "he stedfastly set his face to go to Jerusalem . . ." (Luke 9:51). He heard the voice of inclination; He heard the voice of God. There was no wavering. "He stedfastly set his face." Three elements made up His decision. First, there was commitment. There was no longer any question. The issue was settled. We need to deal honestly, even ruthlessly, with ourselves at this point. It is so easy to drift along without fully making up our minds. And most of our troubles grow out of indecision.

Have you read the book *Quo Vadis?* The title means, "Whither goest thou?" In this fictional story, Peter had failed to convert the Romans and he determined to leave the city. On his way out, Christ appeared to him and said, "Quo vadis?" The question made Peter realize he was turning away from the work he had been called to do. So he turned around and went back, even though it eventually meant a martyr's death. But the point is this: Peter found the peace going back that he had lost running away.

## Courage

Out of commitment comes the second element—courage. Had you looked into the Lord's face as He turned toward Jerusalem, you would have seen no fear. It has been pointed out that we run not because we are afraid; rather we are afraid because we run. Face up to it squarely and honestly; refuse to run. An old ship captain shouted to his sailors during a heavy storm, "Keep her facing it, always facing it, that's the way to get through." With decision comes courage.

"He stedfastly set his face to go to Jerusalem." He made the commitment and then as a result came courage. The two go hand-in-hand. We are afraid only until we fully decide.

## Calmness

As a result of commitment and courage, something else comes—calmness. Even as Christ hung upon the pain-drenched cross, He spoke a calm valedictory: "Father, into thy hands I commend my spirit" (Luke 23:46). I know of no other way to attain calm peace in our own minds and hearts.

Very often I travel by airplane. I always go through the same mental routine: When I sit down and fasten the seat belt, I begin to wonder if the plane will fly. The engines start and I listen to see if they are running smoothly. Slowly the plane begins to move down the runway. The pilot can stop and go back until he reaches a certain point. That point is where the speed is so great that he couldn't stop; he must go on. It is the point of commitment. Then I settle down because there is no turning back. I must put my faith in the plane. And because I believe in the plane, I am not afraid and I feel calm as we fly into the sky.

Several years ago Joshua Liebman wrote *Peace of Mind*. Later Fulton J. Sheen wrote *Peace of Soul*. Since one was Jewish and the other was Catholic, the publisher suggested to Ralph W. Sockman, a Protestant, that he write on the same theme. He did write the book—entitled *How to Believe*. I think he showed keen insight, because when one learns to believe he finds peace of mind and soul.

Because I believe in the airplane, I am willing to commit my life to the principle that it is able to carry me safely on my journey. Likewise, when I believe in God, I commit my life into His hands, believing that He can and will carry me through. And believing in God, being commited to God, I find courage and calmness. So Jesus said, "No man can serve two masters." Make your commitment to God, and He will carry you through life.

Then read what Christ said following that verse: "Therefore I say unto you, Take no thought [be not anxious] for your life . . ." (Matthew 6:25). He points out that we do not need to worry about clothes, food, and the material things of life. Look at the birds of the air and the lilies of the field. God abundantly provides for them; shall He not do much more for one of His own children?

Jesus concluded by saying, "But seek ye first the kingdom of God, and his righteousness . . ." (6:33). Put God first. Decide once and for all on the right. Now notice—Christ doesn't say we will be denied the things we want in life. He says, "All these things shall be added unto you" (6:33). The picture we have that the godly life must be one of hard sacrifice is wrong. The psalmist said, "I have . . . not seen the righteous forsaken . . ." (Psalms 37:25). Come to think of it, I never have either!

## The Peace He Gives

One of the most appealing verses in the Bible is John 14:27, which reads: "Peace I leave with you, my peace I give unto you: not as the world giveth, give I unto you. Let not your heart be troubled, neither let it be afraid." We feel drawn to those words as a thirsty man is drawn to a cool spring. More than anything else in this life we want inner peace. We are tired of living with our inner conflicts, tension, and turmoil; and we would rather possess peace of mind and heart than anything else.

Peace is not something we search for and work for—Jesus said, "My peace I give unto you." He gives it freely. All that remains is for us to accept it. But in order to be able to accept His peace, there are three other things we must accept from Him—His pardon, His Presence, and His purposes. Let's look at each of them.


## His Pardon

First, we must accept His pardon. Some sin we have committed, some wrong of which we are ashamed, is troubling our minds. A sense of guilt haunts us, and we are never able to get away from it. We are sorry for what we have done, we refuse to do it again, and sincerely we ask God to forgive us. God always forgives those who ask Him to and who really mean it. The Bible says, "If we confess our sins, he is faithful and just to forgive us our sins, and to cleanse us from all unrighteousness" (1 John 1:9).

But there is a curious quirk within the human mind that makes it hard for us to accept God's forgiveness. Knowing we have done wrong, we feel we deserve punishment, and we live in constant dread and fear that something bad is going to happen to us. Subconsciously we say, "I've done wrong and someday I will pay for it." I went to the dentist the other day. He didn't hurt me, but I kept expecting him to at any moment. Thus I could never relax as long as I was in his chair. In the same way, the constant dread and fear of some dire punishment for our sins robs life of all chance of deep inner peace.

One way to gain faith in the forgiveness of God is to practice forgiving other people. In fact, this is essential because Jesus said, "For if ye forgive men their trespasses, your heavenly Father will also forgive you" (Matthew 6:14).

In his book *Learning to Have Faith*, Dr. John A. Redhead imagines a man with two buckets, one filled with water and the other with oil. Both are full to the brim. You cannot pour the oil from one bucket into the other because both are full. Also, the two would not mix.

Now, imagine that one of those buckets is you and the other is God. He wants to pour His forgiving love into your life, but you are holding resentment toward some person and thus you have no room for God. Also, God's loving mercy and your unforgiving spirit won't mix. So before you can accept His forgiveness, you must forgive that other person.

"My peace I give unto you," said Christ. Before you can accept His peace, you must first accept His pardon.

Some have come to me in a hopeless condition, feeling they have committed some unpardonable sin. I explain that the only unpardonable sin is to become so hardened by sin that the soul loses its feeling. The very fact that one feels a sense of guilt is positive proof of his ability to receive pardon. So I suggest to such a person that instead of concentrating on his sins, he fill his mind with God's promises to forgive his sins. Note these words: "Him that cometh to me I will in no wise cast out" (John 6:37); "Whosoever believeth in him should not perish, but have everlasting life" (John 3:16); "As far as the east is from the west, so far hath he removed our transgressions from us" (Psalms 103:12); "And Jesus said unto her, Neither do I condemn thee; go, and sin no more" (John 8:11).

Fix these words in your mind: "Him that cometh" . . . "Whosoever" . . . "removed our transgressions from us" . . . "sin no more." Those are God's words to you—accept His forgiveness and believe that you have received it.

## His Presence

Second, to accept His peace, we must accept His Presence. At the beginning of World War II in England, the authorities evacuated the children from the areas under bombardment. But they soon discovered they had made a mistake—the children became emotionally upset. Though they were safe and all their physical necessities were provided for, being deprived of the love and companionship of their parents did them great harm.

So it is with us. We may live in the finest house, eat the best food, and have all the things money can buy. Yet, without the fellowship of our heavenly Father, we remain restless and without inner peace.

The Bible says, "Be still, and know that I am God" (Psalms

46:10). Also, "in quietness and in confidence shall be your strength . . ." (Isaiah 30:15). Stillness—quietness; that is the greatest need of multitudes in the noisy, hurried life of today. Starr Daily, a man who knows much about the art of spiritual healing, made this amazing statement: "No man or woman of my acquaintance who knows how to practice silence and does it has ever been sick to my knowledge."

Surely the practice of silence is more soothing and healing than most medicines. How can one learn the art of stillness, of quietness, of silence? Pascal, the great philosopher, said: "After observing humankind over a long period of years, I came to the conclusion that one of man's great troubles is his inability to be still."

I was on a plane once when the pilot announced over the speaker, "I am now going to cut the motors momentarily to make an adjustment to allow us to climb higher." A man needs to learn to "cut his motor" and to make adjustments if he wants the ability to climb higher. There is tremendous power to be gained from completely silencing the mind, but it isn't easy to do. Here is one way to accomplish it: Go alone to the quietest place available to you. Do not read. Do not write. Begin by letting a mental picture of the most peaceful scene you have ever witnessed pass across your mind. Some months ago, I spent two weeks at Sea Island. Under the spell of that lovely place, every bit of the tension and hurry of life was drained out of me and I became completely relaxed. But for me, the benefits of Sea Island are not limited to the actual days I was there. I enjoy that experience again and again as I sit quietly and begin to see in my mind the ocean, the waves rolling up on the beach and back again, the gentle swaying of the sea grass. Through the power of imagination, one can quickly transport himself back into a peaceful scene and experience its healing influence.

Then, under that spell, begin to repeat audibly some peaceful words. Words have great suggestive power. Speak words like earthquake, murder, house on fire, cancer, blood—and you feel nervousness. But words like tranquility, serenity, imperturbable—such words create within you the mood they describe. Repeat them aloud, slowly and thoughtfully.

Have you ever dropped a pebble into a very still pond and watched the tiny waves go out over the surface of the water? When your mind is quiet, drop into it some of the great truths of God from the Bible, such as: "The Lord is my shepherd; I shall not want" (Psalms 23:1); "Let not your heart be troubled: ye believe in God, believe also in me" (John 14:1); "The eternal God is thy refuge, and underneath are the everlasting arms . . ." (Deuteronomy 33:27).

Usually at this moment I will recall a few lines of some of the hymns I love:

*What a friend we have in Jesus*
*All our sins and griefs to bear. . . .*


*Jesus calls us, o'er the tumult*
*Of our life's wild, restless sea,*
*Day by day His sweet voice soundeth,*
*Saying, "Christian follow Me."*


## His Purposes

After realizing God's pardon and experiencing His Presence, you then must take the third step necessary to accepting His peace: accept God's purposes. One of the primary causes of inner tension is mental disorganization. We need to learn the advantages of taking one thing at a time and concentrating on it. And above the daily routine of life, we need guiding goals and purposes.

Remember Christ's experience at the Garden of Gethsemane: He got Himself away from the crowds—even away from His closest friends. After He got quiet and alone with God, He then said, "Nevertheless, not my will, but thine, be done" (Luke 22:42). Who doubts but that in this moment all the inner strain and tension left Him?

More than anything, people want inner peace—peace of mind and peace of heart. We seek this in many ways, but there is really only one way to find inner peace. The great and wise Dante said it this way: "In His will is our peace." I am reminded of these words when I visit the rock at the Garden of Gethsemane where Jesus prayed, "Nevertheless, not my will, but thine, be done." I have often wondered why that complete surrender to the will of God brings such happy peace into our lives. When I contemplate it, I think of four reasons why we find peace through accepting God's will for our lives:

1. It takes away the fear of getting lost in life. I was once in a small two-seater airplane with a friend of mine, flying across the

country. He did not have a radio in the plane to guide it. He was visually following his way. Suddenly he said to me that he was lost. There were no landmarks he recognized; the ground below was rough, and there was no place to land. There was some fear of running out of gasoline, and for me, there followed some very uncomfortable moments. Finally he saw something he recognized and got back on course toward our landing field. Being lost—not knowing the way—can cause very real fear.

It is fascinating to study the migration of the Pacific Golden Plover. These birds are hatched in the northlands of Alaska and Siberia. Before the young ones are old enough to fly great distances, the old birds desert them and fly far away to the Hawaiian Islands. The young birds are left behind to grow strong enough to follow their parents.

One day these birds rise into the sky and set their course out over the Pacific. They have never made that journey before, and they must cross 2,000 miles of ocean with no marks to guide them. During this trip they have not even one opportunity to stop for rest or food, and frequently they encounter high winds and storms. Yet unerringly they fly straight to those tiny specks in the Pacific, the Hawaiian Islands.

How do you explain the flight of those birds? Surely God has provided for those birds something akin to our radio beams—something they can follow without getting lost. I firmly believe God has made the same provisions for mankind. When our lives are in harmony with His will, even though we cannot see the way ahead, we have an instinctive sense of the right direction. With courage and confidence, we move steadily ahead through life without any fear of getting lost, knowing that through the storms and uncertainties, we shall come to the right place at last. That is a wonderful assurance to possess. "In all thy ways acknowledge him, and he shall direct thy paths" (Proverbs 3:6).

2. A second reason why "In His will is our peace" is true is that it relieves us of the burden of the responsibilities of tomorrow. If you will study your fears and worries, you will see that most of them are not concerned with the failures and mistakes of yesterday, because you can usually overcome those. Neither are most of your fears and worries about the things of the present, because you know you can make it through the day. But when you turn your face toward the dim unknown of tomorrow and you are not sure what lies in your path, you often worry and become afraid.

When God asks us to follow His will, He is saying, "I will accept the responsibility for your future." After Jesus had said on the cross, "It is finished," He then said, "Father, into thy hands I commend my spirit" (John 19:30, Luke 23:46). It was a cry of faith. He had done His best; He had given His all. Now He was willing to leave the results in God's hands.

Because we have faith in God, we can say with the hymn writer:

> *Keep thou my feet; I do not ask to see*
> *The distant scene—one step enough for me.*

God usually does not make known His will to us for years ahead. Instead He shows us one step at a time, and as we take the step we know it leads us much closer to the very best possible life there is for each of us. Whatever occurs to us in life is not our responsibility; it is God's will, and thus we need have no fear. Some will face great tragedies. Others must face the untimely death of a loved one, a physical deformity, a bitter disappointment that seems impossible to correct. But the completion and fulfillment of God's will is not limited to this life here on earth. He plans in terms of eternity, and though God may seem defeated, let us reserve our judgment until the complete story is written.

3. Another way in which God's will brings us peace is by eliminating the conflicts within our lives. Instead of squandering our energies with countless decisions, wondering whether to do this or that, we can settle it with one great decision: "I shall do the will of God." This attitude brings into our lives a singleness of purpose that provides peace and strength. We remember how Paul said, "This *one* thing I do." When we reach that point, most problems and decisions of life are solved. When we accept the will of God, we instinctively know when the right choice comes along.

Dedication to the will of God therefore eliminates the conflict between right and wrong. A man came in to see me some time ago about a wrong in his life. He knew that what he was doing was wrong, but he didn't want to give it up. The resulting conflict had made him miserable and unhappy. If we submit to God's will, we know that what we do is right. And this leads to the next reason.

4. "In His will is our peace" is also true because when we follow God's will, we have the approval of a good conscience. I know that conscience is a difficult thing to explain, but after the psychologists have said all they can say in explaining the human conscience— and some of them explain it away completely—we still recognize it as a voice within saying, "This is right; that is wrong." But

whatever a conscience is, it must be trained and developed. This is very important because some people have done cruel and evil things believing that they were following the dictates of their consciences.

If we feel we have done something wrong, we may argue with our consciences and say, "Everybody else is doing it." But we cannot be completely at peace until we have made it right. Huckleberry Finn was right when he said, "Conscience takes up more room than all the rest of a fellow's insides." When we do what God wants us to do, we feel mighty good inside.

I cherish many of the stories my father told me about his own life. There is one in particular that I think bothered him all his life. I remember he told it with sadness in his voice. When he was a boy growing up in the north Georgia mountains of White County, life was simple and his family did not have many things. More than anything else, he wanted a Barlow knife.

One day his father was going to Gainesville and he told him to clean off a certain creek bank while he was away. For doing that job, he would buy my father the Barlow knife he wanted so badly. Eagerly my father set out to do the work in happy anticipation of his father's return when he would receive his blessed reward. When he got down to the creek, however, the weather was hot and the water was so inviting he decided to take a short swim. Playing in the water, the time passed swiftly. But then, there was no special hurry—it took a long time for a wagon to go from Loudsville to Gainesville and back. He would easily get the work finished tomorrow.

The next day, as he started his work, he happened to see some little fish jumping in the creek. It would do no harm to catch a few, so he dug up some bait and fished while the fish were biting. Again the hours sped by until the chance to get his job done was gone.

That night his father would be coming home. Faithful to his promise, he would have that prized Barlow knife. But that boy was now very unhappy. He would have to face his father and say, "I didn't do the job. I didn't earn the knife."

But what a contrast when we think of our Lord. He had many temptations to turn Him aside, to waste His time and His life. In faithfully following His Father's will, often the going was hard. But one day He "lifted up his eyes to heaven, and said, . . . I have finished the work which thou gavest me to do" (John 17:1, 4). As

He hung on the cross again He said, "It is finished . . ." (John 19:30).

God has given us certain tasks in life. When we follow God's will, we can complete our tasks and earn our reward. And I know of no greater happiness we can experience than to know we can face God and say, "I've done my best." Truly, "in His will is our peace!"

## Peace Robbers

The elder friend of Rabbi Liebman was certainly right when he told him that the most important possession of all is "peace of mind." Even if one has health, love, beauty, talent, power, riches, and fame—the essentials that the Rabbi listed as a young man—still, if he lacks "peace of mind," life is a hideous torment and an intolerable burden.

I have found that there are four main reasons why so many people do not have this blessed inner peace:

1. We worry about the things we do not have and thereby become dissatisfied with the things we do have. Once I was the pastor of a little church far back in the mountains. There was an old man in the community with whom I spent a lot of time and from whom I learned a lot. He was a wise philosopher and he would tell me of life as it used to be—how very little the people had, yet how happy they were.

But one day the mailman left a mail-order catalog at a neighbor's house. The people began to look at it, first wonderingly and then longingly. Soon every home in the community had one of the catalogs. The old man would sadly shake his head as he told me how they turned away from the things that used to mean so much as they turned the pages of the catalog, and forgot the beauty of the mountains around them when they thought of the many things they did not possess.

On his eightieth birthday, someone asked Bishop Herbert Welch the secret of his serene spirit. He replied, "As I grow older, life becomes simpler because I see the essentials more clearly in the evening light."

2. We have developed a "crisis psychology." Some crisis is always coming along, such as a debt or a sickness or a war or a thousand other things and, before we realize it, life is one constant crisis.

The great singer Enrico Caruso had a dinner table trick which he used frequently. He would hold a slender glass high in the air and sing an ascending scale until he came to a high note which he would hold until the constant vibration shattered the glass. And one crisis after another in a life will shatter it. John Greenleaf Whittier prayed,

> *Take from our souls the strain and stress,*
> *And let our ordered lives confess*
> *The beauty of thy peace.*

We must learn not to make a crisis out of every unhappy experience that comes along.

3. Our inner conflicts destroy our inner peace. Man is made with a higher nature and a lower nature, and there is a constant struggle between the two. Jesus had perfect inner peace because He was perfectly good.

I suppose that if a person were completely bad, he would have a false sense of peace. Sometimes we think we can get rid of our inner conflicts by squelching our higher nature and living on the lower animal level. The prodigal son tried that but eventually his longing for home destroyed all possibility of happiness in the hog pen. Augustine, as a young man, tried to find peace in every form of sensual indulgence. Eventually, he had to come back to God, saying, "Our souls are restless until they find their rest in Thee."

4. There are conflicts between ourselves and other people that destroy our peace. We have had our feelings hurt. We carry a grudge. We have an unforgiving spirit. Someone has suggested that instead of praying, "Forgive us our trespasses, as we forgive those who trespass against us," we should pray, "Forgive me my trespasses as I forgive _____ for what he has done to me." There is marvelous power in a personal prayer like that.

> And the peace of God, which passeth all understanding, shall keep your hearts and minds through Christ Jesus (Philippians 4:7).

## Fret Not Thyself

The first words of the Thirty-seventh Psalm are these: "Fret not thyself. . . ." We tend to blame our troubles and our worries on the circumstances of life or on what someone else has done to us.

The truth of the matter is, most of our inner unhappiness results from our fretting ourselves.

There is nothing sweeter on this earth than a little baby. However sometimes something hurts the little baby, or it becomes thirsty or hungry or cold or uncomfortable. Then the baby does not face life in a gallant fashion; instead the baby begins to howl and scream at the top of its voice. What happens when a baby cries? It simply acts like a baby; it hasn't yet learned to cope with unhappiness. The psalmist's words "Fret not thyself" say that when we are uncomfortable, or when we are hurting, let's not act like babies. Babies never do anything to help themselves. Those who are really grown-up do not spend their energies in whining, fussing, and worrying. They seek to discover the trouble and do what is necessary to remedy it.

Why do we fret ourselves? Why do we worry? Let me give six reasons:

1. When we are tired and worn out physically, it is much easier to feel uncomfortable and unhappy. So in every life there must be some sort of restful change. Once a preacher announced that he was going to take a vacation. One of the members of the church said, "The devil never takes a vacation." The minister replied, "That is the reason he is the devil."

Every person needs to discover some form of recreation that leads to relaxation. One can play golf, fish, read, watch television, travel—there are many things to do, but there are times when we need to get our minds off of ourselves and our daily living.

2. We fret ourselves because something hurts us. I know a football coach who says to his players at the beginning of the season, "If you expect to play football, you must expect sometime to get hit and to get hurt." The same thing is true of life. If we expect to live, it is a certainty that somewhere along the way of life we are going to get hurt.

There are three main ways that people get hurt. Sometimes we are hurt because of a severe loss. We feel the pinch of poverty, the loss of health, our ambitions are thwarted, a friendship is broken—there are many ways to lose in life.

Sometimes we are hurt because of what life withholds from us. Struggle and strive as we may, the best prizes often elude us. Our finest dreams fail to come true.

Hope is a wonderful thing, but continued unrealized hope can break our hearts. There are those who feel near to the sunset of life, yet they see themselves no nearer to the castle of their dreams than when they started. That hurts.

Finally, sometimes we are bothered by what happens to other people. We suffer in sympathy because a loved one suffers. Or we are jealous of the success of others and become envious.

3. We worry because we refuse to accept life as it is. Some things in life are fixed; they cannot be changed or avoided. Instead of accepting them bravely and courageously, we whine and fret and rebel. People often complain about the weather, but there is not much any of us can do about it. Someone once described it this way:

*After all, man is nothing but a fool,*
*When it's hot, he wants it cool.*
*When it's cool, he wants it hot;*
*He always wants it the way it's not.*

We need to remember that there are some things that we cannot change, but we must accept them and make the best of them.

Failure and success both exist in life, and sooner or later we expect to get a taste of both of them. A blessed, happy person does his or her best and leaves the rest and does not worry. We all have limitations. Every so often we hear somebody say, "I can do anything anybody else can do." That is a stupid and untrue statement. No person can do everything that everybody else can do. God did not put all the stars in any one person's sky. God did not plant all the flowers in any one person's garden. But God gave to every person *some* stars and *some* flowers, and we find happiness in life with what we have.

4. We become upset when we are too self-centered. Jesus never worried about anything. It is almost a sacrilege to ever think of Him fretting or fussing or worrying, because His mind and heart were set on something greater than His own life. When soldiers are in combat, putting everything they have into it, they often become so preoccupied with fighting that they fail to notice their own wounds. When we become less self-centered and become more cause-centered, then our worries disappear.

5. Fear strikes us down when we are at war with our own consciences. Life can become divided. We face decisions we dare not make. We hear calls we dare not answer. We see paths of duty we dare not follow. Tremendous power lies in decision.

I have spent many nights in a beautiful hotel on the Mount of

Olives in Israel. Down below is the Garden of Gethsemane. Many times I get up early before breakfast and walk down that hill to that garden. I look at those olive trees where the disciples slept, and inside that beautiful church is that rock where Jesus might have prayed. It was not easy for Him. The Bible says, "His sweat was as it were great drops of blood falling down to the ground" (Luke 22:44). But during that period He made His decision, "Nevertheless, not my will, but thine, be done" (Luke 22:42).

There is tremendous power in decisions, and some worried, unhappy, fretful people cannot make up their minds. There comes a time when we must say, "This one thing I do."

6. The supreme cause of self-fretting and worry is lack of faith in God. Let us turn back to the Thirty-seventh Psalm, which begins, "Fret not thyself . . ." Consider this list of phrases from that psalm:

- Trust in the Lord (verse 3)
- Delight thyself also in the Lord (verse 4)
- Commit thy way unto the Lord (verse 5)
- Those that wait upon the Lord, they shall inherit the earth (verse 9)
- The Lord upholdeth the righteous (verse 17)
- I have been young, and now am old; yet have I not seen the righteous forsaken, nor his seed begging bread (verse 25)
- Behold the upright: for the end of that man is peace (verse 37)
- And the Lord shall help them, and deliver them . . . from the wicked, and save them, because they trust in him (verse 40)

The psalmist is saying, "If you will trust in God, you do not have anything to worry about." Vital faith and worry are incompatible.

## You Can Possess Peace

One of the most poignant stories in all of literature is the one about King David's infant son who was sick. It is found in 2 Samuel 12:15–23. The son that Uriah's wife bore David was stricken. David prayed that the child be saved. He even fasted and "lay all night upon the earth" (verse 16). Friends and servants went out to him to get him to get up from the earth and come into the house. He would not get up, and he would eat nothing. For seven days this went on and then the child died. His servants were afraid to tell

David that the child was dead, because they were afraid of what he might do to himself when he heard the news. When David heard the servants whispering, he knew in his heart that the child had died. Thus, David asked the servants, "Is the child dead?" They replied, "He is dead."

Then David rose up from the ground, went in and took a bath, changed his clothes and went to the church and worshipped. When he came home, he sat down at the table to eat. The servants were really surprised at his actions. They reminded him how he fasted and wept for the child while it was alive, but now that the child was dead, he ceased weeping and would eat.

David explained, "While the child was yet alive, I fasted and wept: for I said, Who can tell whether God will be gracious to me, that the child may live? But now he is dead, wherefore should I fast? Can I bring him back again? I shall go to him, but he shall not return to me" (2 Samuel 12:22,23).

This is a marvelous example for every one of us who has had a crisis and especially a death in the family. It is even a marvelous example for facing one's own death. As long as there was life, David did everything he possibly could. When death came, instead of cursing God, instead of drowning himself in sorrow, instead of saying, "Why . . . why . . . why?," he accepted the fact that nothing could be done. He had done his best; now it was time to look to the future and go on. So, he could bathe, eat his dinner, and begin to think about tomorrow. There is marvelous power and peace in acceptance. David accepted death without reservation.

## Accept What Has Happened

Once on a vacation trip, my wife and I were driving through a desert in the western part of the United States. It was my habit to carry my money in a clip in my pants pocket. For some reason, I put my hand in that pocket and discovered my money was gone! I stopped the car, and we got out and searched thoroughly behind the seat and throughout the car. I felt in all of my pockets. I even opened my suitcase and went through that, and I looked in the pockets of clothes I had worn the day before, but the money was not to be found. I sat there bemoaning our loss and then my wife said, "Are we just going to sit here in the desert worrying about what we have lost, or are we going to go on?" So, I started the car and we continued the trip. We were able to work things out and had a good trip.

Since that experience, there have been several occasions when life did not go for me as I had planned. When I had a problem to worry about, the thought would come to me, "Am I going to just sit here in the desert worrying, or am I going to go on?" There are some times in every life when we need to stop worrying and start going again. We need to accept what has happened, but we realize it is not the end of our world.

I once had the high privilege of visiting with Pope Paul VI. He was the only pope with whom I had any personal contact, thus when he died, it had special meaning for me. I read with interest all the accounts of his funeral. When he was buried, there began a specified period of mourning, which came to an end after a specified number of days. Then the cardinals began their meeting to elect a new pope. The many people who loved Pope Paul VI will continue to hold him in their hearts, but they will also accept the new pope and the Catholic church will continue its work. So it is in life, we accept and then we keep going. Acceptance and peace go together. One leads to the other.

One of the Bible verses which is well-known to many of us is Isaiah 26:3: "Thou wilt keep him in perfect peace, whose mind is stayed on thee: because he trusteth in thee." There is a beautiful melody and great inspiration in these words: *perfect peace*.

## Empty Your Mind

This verse brings to mind two actions we need to take. First, we need to empty our minds. I live in a house which has a large attic. It is so convenient to put things in the attic, and over the years I have accumulated a vast number of articles—some of them worthless and useless. I keep telling myself that I need to clean out my attic and give to some charitable organization all those articles that I cannot use. But somehow I keep putting it off. I suspect that there are many attics that need to be cleaned out. Wouldn't it be a wonderful thing if we could clean out our minds as we can clean out our attics? Or wash out our minds as we can wash our hands?

After Rabbi Joshua Liebman wrote his book *Peace of Mind*, he was swamped with letters from people seeking that peace. His mail was heavy; his telephone rang constantly; many people came to see him. He was a young, kindhearted rabbi, only thirty-eight years old. He tried to help every person and he died in just three years at the age of forty-one. He just could not stand up to the burden. But before he died, he said, "I am appalled at the multitude of people who have never learned to empty their minds."

There are two types of unfamiliar hymns. One is the hymn that we have never heard or sung before. The other kind of unfamiliar hymn is the one we have sung so many times that whenever we sing it, we never think about it. The words have become meaningless. Many of us have sung "What a Friend We Have in Jesus" since we were children. We sing it without thinking. If we would sing it thoughtfully, it could literally change our lives. The first verse is especially helpful. As you read it, think about what it says:

> What a friend we have in Jesus,
> All our sins and griefs to bear!
> What a privilege to carry
> Everything to God in prayer!
> O what peace we often forfeit,
> O what needless pain we bear,
> All because we do not carry
> Everything to God in prayer!

As we look back over our lives, we can remember hurts, losses, mistakes, wrongs, and other deeds that we have done. We also remember acts that have been done by others to us and against us. Jesus will bear these burdens if we take them to Him in prayer.

Once a sixty-three-year-old lady phoned me to say that she was sick and expected to die rather soon. She told me that before she died she wanted something settled. She told me that when she was twenty years old, she stole ten dollars out of the cash register of a store where she worked. She wanted to send the ten dollars to me and let me return it to the store. Of course, I helped her in every way I could, but imagine the burden of guilt that she had carried for forty-three years for only ten dollars! Why, in the name of common sense, did she not settle it many years ago? And why, in the name of common sense, do not all of us settle some things and, like David, "get up and wash our faces" and go on?

## Fill Your Mind

The prophet Isaiah promised that "perfect peace" would be the possession of those "whose mind is stayed on thee." I have said that we need to empty our minds of a lot of things. We also need to fill our minds with the right things. Too many of us concentrate on our troubles instead of our triumphs—our problems instead of our powers—our fears instead of our faith—our sins instead of our Saviour.

Once I heard a lady relate that whenever she went to bed at night, the worries of life would crowd in upon her and she would toss and turn until finally, out of sheer exhaustion, she would go to sleep. In the morning, she would wake up tired and nervous. Then one day, she heard or read of a better idea and she began to practice it with marvelous results. One of her greatest joys was arranging flowers in a vase. She especially liked red roses. When she went to bed at night, she began to picture in her mind a table with two dozen beautiful red roses upon it. In the center of the table she imagined a vase, then mentally, she began picking up the roses one by one and arranging them in the vase. Usually, she would be asleep before she got all the roses arranged. That simple little procedure did marvelous things for her.

Here is one of the most psychologically potent statements in all the Bible: "Finally, brethren, whatever is true, whatever is honorable, whatever is just, whatever is pure, whatever is lovely, whatever is gracious, if there is any excellence, if there is anything worthy of praise, think about these things" (Philippians 4:8 RSV).

Every so often, I am reminded of the song which says, "When you are discouraged, thinking all is lost. . . ." Sooner or later, most of us will have that experience. It is then when we need to remember the next line of that song which is, "Count your many blessings, name them one by one." The Prophet Isaiah said that "perfect peace" is brought about with what we allow to fill our minds. It is good to think about beautiful things and our blessings, but the greatest power comes when we begin to fill our minds with God. That is what Isaiah meant when he said: "whose mind is stayed on thee."

I recently had a heavy burden on my heart. I could not deal with it as I wanted to, and it worried me considerably. One night I called a close minister friend and said to him, "Would you pray right now over the phone about this problem on my behalf?" As he prayed fervently and sincerely, the answer came. I felt a confidence and a joy and a peace. The problem was not a burden any longer. I believe that in that certain circumstance I needed some extra help in letting God become completely dominant in my thinking in reference to that problem. I felt that the answer had come, and I felt completely at ease and at peace.

## Penicillin for Despair

Abbé Pierre has a phrase—"penicillin for despair." He declares that to be the world's greatest need. I am inclined to agree. Every person who has been plagued by anxious fears feels the need of "penicillin for despair." Certainly Christ felt that need. As He knelt that night in Gethsemane, the Bible says, He "began to be sore amazed, and to be very heavy" (Mark 14:33). The Revised Version translates that to read that He "began to be greatly amazed, and sore troubled" (RV). Moffatt's translation gives, "he began to feel appalled and agitated" (MOFFATT).

Vincent Taylor, a renowned scholar of the Greek language, says, "Those verbs denote distress which follows a great shock." He points out that hundreds and thousands of British people are still suffering from the shock of the last world war, though many of them do not realize it. Likewise, there are many in America who are still suffering from the shock of that war. And there are numerous other shocks that have come into the personal lives of people.

I have had many people talk to me about how they went to bed only to toss and turn for hours before sleep came; others told of how they suddenly began to tremble, or break into a cold sweat, or feel constant fatigue, or have an abnormal dryness in the mouth, a palpitating heart, a constant headache, or a deadness of feeling when they seemed to lose ability to love their own family and even God. Some have even told me about inclinations to attempt suicide.

For people who know the sufferings brought by anxious fears, I have deep sympathy. I have had some of those same feelings. Nearly every normal person has at some time been very heavy—greatly distressed—troubled—appalled—agitated. Some people seem condemned to live with anxiety as a constant companion.

In times of anxious strain we are often told to "have faith" and all our troubles will magically disappear. That is simply not true. Jesus had faith, but He also knew the meaning of naked terror. Some of the greatest saints have cried out for a "penicillin for despair," yet they also had faith. We are told that our fears are imaginary. That is a misstatement. All fears are real—none are imaginary. It may be that imagination caused our fears, or it may be that we reacted in the wrong way to some circumstance of life, but the fears themselves are not imaginary. We are told to "pull ourselves together," but we are not sure what that means. Many do not feel they have strength enough to pull even if they knew what to pull on.

When you feel despair, deep anxiety, trembling fear, or nervous strain, what attitude should you take toward it? Take a look at Mark 14:32–36. Examine the experience of Christ when He felt "very heavy."

We know that Christ was God and that as God He had supernatural insight and power. But Christ was also man, and as a man He experienced our same hungers and thirsts. He endured real temptation. He had human desires. Also, He had experiences of deep anxiety and despair.

Thus we know that anxious fears may come even though one does have faith. We should not feel ashamed because of nervous symptoms. These experiences come to nearly everyone. But there is such a thing as "penicillin for despair." It isn't a pill or a shot in the arm; it is an action or a series of actions. In His moment of despair, Christ did these three things:

1. *He got alone.* That night in Gethsemane He moved a distance from the crowd and took with Him His three closest friends. There are times when it is good for us to be with crowds. There are other times when we need to be with some trusted and close friends. Jesus, no doubt, talked with these three about His troubles. Often that helps. It is wonderful to have a friend to share our deepest thoughts. Often it helps to talk with a minister or a competent counselor. But then Jesus went still further alone. It is important that we see this.

When one is in some dark valley, his first impulse is to tell his troubles to every person who will listen. The reason we want to tell our troubles is because we want sympathy; we get soothing satisfaction from the pity of others and from self-pity. We might deny this, but it is true nonetheless. But the more we talk about our troubles, the worse they become. Speech has a much greater effect on the emotions than thinking has. We can talk about ourselves into almost anything, and the more we talk about our troubles, the worse they seem to us. That's why Jesus got alone—away from the sympathy of others.

2. *He looked to God.* "And he said, Abba, Father, all things are possible unto thee . . ." (Mark 14:36). He took His mind off Himself, and that does much to relieve one of anxiety and fear. But it is hard to do because part of the mind wants to hold onto its worries and despair. That is the easiest way out. To despair is to lose hope, and to lose hope is to give up and quit.

Frequently, we translate our despair into bodily illness. Maybe we don't become invalids, but we never "feel well." Much of the sickness of people is merely an escape from reality, the easiest way out. But this is never a final solution. Deep down we are ashamed of our cowardice. We feel guilty for selling our courage to buy sympathy. But when one looks into the face of God, he has hope because he knows that "all things are possible unto" Him.

3. *He took positive action.* In the midst of despair, the great temptation is to retire, to slip into illness, to surrender. It is a great struggle to do something. It was a struggle for our Lord. Luke vividly portrays the strain Christ was under. He says, "His sweat was as it were great drops of blood falling down to the ground" (Luke 22:44). But in spite of the struggle, Jesus centered His mind on something to do. He refused to withdraw into Himself.

Activity is often the best cure for the blues. Physicians tell us that our fear thoughts come from the higher brain centers while physical activity comes from the lower brain centers. When one begins to exercise those lower brain centers through activity, it lessens the tension of the upper brain centers. I have read of operations in which certain parts of the brain are removed to lessen those fear thoughts. I knew of a man who had a better way—he had daily exercise. He said it "straightened out his thoughts."

What did Jesus do? He prayed, "not my will, but thine, be done." He committed Himself wholly to the will of God. This kind of faith is the answer to fear. It lifts one's thoughts away from his own troubles and centers his mind on the strength of God. It has been truly said, "In His will is our peace." That is the "penicillin for despair." Dedication to His will enables us to say with the psalmist, "Yea, though I walk through the valley of the shadow of death, I will fear no evil: for thou art with me . . ." (Psalms 23:4). Realizing that He is with us, we have confidence that we will get through even the worst experience. Thus there is no room in our minds for despair.

## Do Not Worry About Tomorrow

In regard to the anxiety which leads to morbid worry and fear, Jesus did not content Himself with saying merely, "Do not be anxious." Instead, He gave us two ways to overcome this destructive anxiety. The first way was when He said, "Take therefore no thought for the morrow . . ." (Matthew 6:34). The key word is *therefore.* By that He meant that we are not orphans in the world. In

Matthew 6:26–30, Jesus gave two illustrations: One was the birds of the air. The other was the lilies of the field. Jesus asks each of us if we are not more important than a bird or a flower that will soon die and never live again. And if God cares for the birds—even noting the fall of each one—and if He so beautifully clothes the lilies, then how much more, Jesus says, will God do for one of His own children, made in His image?

The other way we can keep from worrying about tomorrow is found in the second part of Matthew 6:34: "For the morrow shall take thought for the things of itself. Sufficient unto the day is the evil thereof." In other words, we should live one day at a time. I like Moffat's translation of these words: "So never be troubled about tomorrow; tomorrow will take care of itself. The day's own trouble is enough for the day" (MOFFATT).

Robert Quillen told of a famous old naturalist who began to cut trees to build a log house. A friend said, "Isn't that a big undertaking for a man of your years?" The old naturalist replied, "It would be if I thought of chopping the trees, sawing the logs, skinning the bark, laying the foundation, erecting the walls, and putting on the roof. Carrying the load all at once would exhaust me. But it isn't so hard to cut down this one tree and that is all I have to do today."

Sir William Osler, a famous physician and professor of medicine at Johns Hopkins University, tells of one night when he was worried sick. His final examination was coming up the next day, and he was anxious not only about that but also about his future. That night he picked up a copy of Carlyle's works and happened to read this familiar sentence: "Our main business is not to see what lies dimly at a distance, but to do what lies clearly at hand." Years later, when he returned to his native England to be knighted by the king, he said, "More than anything else I owe whatever success I have had to the power of settling down to the day's work and doing it to the best of my ability, letting the future take care of itself."

Isn't it true that most of our worries are borrowed from some other day? We worry about mountains we will never have to climb, about streams we will never have to cross, about situations we will never have to meet. I refer often to the women going to the tomb of Jesus that first Easter morning. It must have been a glorious time, with the sun just rising in majestic splendor, the crisp, cool early spring air, and the lovely wild flowers growing along the way. But they missed all that. Instead, they were worrying about who would roll the stone away. Yet, when they got there, they found the stone had already been rolled away! All their worry was over a situation which had been taken care of before they reached it.

We must remember also that living a day at a time refers just as much to yesterday as it does to tomorrow. God is far more ready to forgive us than we are to forgive ourselves. Suppose you made a mistake yesterday—do you expect to keep the shadow hanging over you for the rest of your life? If you can correct the wrong, then do so and go ahead about the business of living today.

So the two cures for worrying about tomorrow are, first, put your trust in the God who made both you and this world, and second, put your best into living this one day, realizing that step by step He will carry you through. Three sentences from Paul also express this faith: "If God be for us, who can be against us?" (Romans 8:31). "My God shall supply all your need . . . (Philippians 4:19). "All things work together for good to them that love God . . ." (Romans 8:28).

## Let the Peace of God Rule in Your Hearts

Oftentimes when I feel tired or tense or worried or frightened, I get great comfort out of quoting to myself, six or eight times, these words of Paul, "And let the peace of God rule in your hearts . . ." (Colossians 3:15). To say those words over and over makes me feel good and relaxed. Too many times our hearts are ruled by turmoil instead of peace. Nervous tension can wreak havoc on human personalities and bodies. There is no way of escaping the vicissitudes of human existence. But when the peace of God rules within our hearts, we feel confident and supreme. It was William Cullen Bryant who wrote:

> He who, from zone to zone,
> Guides through the boundless sky thy certain flight,
> In the long way that I must tread alone,
> Will lead my steps aright.

Robert Louis Stevenson said it this way: "Quiet minds cannot be perplexed or frightened but go on in fortune or in misfortune at their own private pace like the ticking of a clock during a thunderstorm." That is a beautiful analogy. No matter how hard the wind blows or how loud the thunder crashes, the clock does not change its pace. It keeps its same steady *ticktock, ticktock, ticktock*.

I get a new thrill every time I read Captain Eddie Rickenbacker's story of three awful weeks on a little raft lost in the far Pacific. When asked how they were able to endure that experience, his simple, unaffected explanation was: "We prayed." For days they had drifted helplessly under the scorching tropic sun. Their feet became blistered, their faces burned, their mouths and bodies parched. The heat, the hunger, the exhaustion, brought them to the breaking point. The men with him were young and inexperienced, facing their first great trial. But Eddie Rickenbacker believed in prayer. He had learned to pray at his mother's knee, and in all the crises of his life, prayer had given him the comfort and courage he needed. On the eighth day of hunger and thirst and fear, some of the men were alarmingly desperate. That day they read these words from the New Testament: "Take no thought for your life, what ye shall eat, or what ye shall drink; nor yet for your body, what ye shall put on. . . . But seek ye first the kingdom of God, and his righteousness; and all these things shall be added unto you" (Matthew 6:25, 33). And they prayed.

What happened next seemed like a miracle, and who can say it was not? A sea gull flew in out of nowhere and landed on Rickenbacker's head. They had food. Also they had bait for two fishhooks they had. Then came their first rainstorm, and they had water. From then on they prayed with renewed confidence. They calmed down because they believed God was with them.

They continued to drift for nearly two weeks, but they continued to believe. On the twenty-first day they were spotted by a plane. It was truly a miraculous rescue, for the rafts were tiny little dots on the vast surface of the ocean. To be seen, a plane had to fly almost directly above them. And in answer to everybody, Rickenbacker simply said, "We prayed."

Affirm to yourself, "The peace of God is ruling in my heart." Say it again and again until it becomes fixed in your thinking. Then go on with your activities, but pause frequently to say, "The peace of God is ruling in my heart." Keep it up day by day, and you will see that God's ruling will bring you quiet calmness and power.

## Acquaint Yourself with Him and Be at Peace

Every year we see marvelous and wonderful progress in the field of medical science. At one time diphtheria was one of the dreaded diseases of mankind. But in America today, nobody is afraid of diphtheria; it has practically been eliminated. So has smallpox, and, thank God, so has polio. Pneumonia also used to be a dreaded disease, but today, physicians have medicines that can deal with pneumonia. Now great progress is being made in the field of cancer.

Medical science marches on to new heights. However, in spite of all the great progress in medicine, our doctors' offices are more crowded today than ever before. Perhaps much of the illness of today is in our minds. Maybe we do not make too much progress in the areas of worry, fear, stress, overwork and underrest, alcohol, diet, anxiety and tension, and such things. We thank God for the medicines that protect our bodies from the enemies that would destroy them. But we need more than medicine for the protection of our minds.

Instead of looking for something new, we might go back to one of the oldest books ever written—the Book of Job in the Bible. What we need to protect our minds is found in Job 22:21: "Acquaint now thyself with him, and be at peace. . . ." Although thousands of years old, that's still good advice in our worried, fast-moving society today. Most of us are better acquainted with our troubles than we are with God. However, as I read this suggestion in Job 22, I find listed there seven marvelous results for anyone who does acquaint himself with God:

1. "Good shall come unto thee" (verse 21). That does not mean that *everything* that happens will be good. It does mean that when we become acquainted with God, there comes into our lives a special quality and strength that somehow ultimately brings good to us.
2. "Thou shalt be built up" (verse 23). Here God promises both physical healing and lifted spirits—a new strength, power, and vitality.
3. "Then shalt thou lay up gold" (verse 24). It is so easy to become worried about finances. We live in a world where material needs are very real. God created all wealth there is and He still controls it, so then what do we have to worry about?
4. "Then shalt thou have thy delight in the Almighty" (verse 26). When one says, "I am delighted," it means joy and satisfaction; it means peace and happiness. What a wonderful state in which to live!

5. "Thou shalt also decree a thing, and it shall be established unto thee" (verse 28). That is, you will not be defeated and frustrated any longer. You will know what it means to succeed at something you want to accomplish.
6. "Light shall shine upon thy ways" (verse 28). Instead of stumbling along in darkness and groping in the haze of fear, you will see a way in which you can walk.
7. "When men are cast down, then thou shalt say, There is lifting up" (verse 29). Though life has a way of knocking us down, it cannot keep us down.

How are these seven things accomplished? Let us read again, "Acquaint now thyself with him." As we saturate our minds with the power, the goodness, and the love of God, these seven things will happen to us. The twenty-second chapter of the Book of Job is truly an inspiration!

## Control Your Emotions

To get ahead in life and to be happy, you must learn to *control your emotions*. Here are four simple suggestions that will work wonders for all who try them.

1. *Study yourself* and determine your weak spots. Achilles had a vulnerable heel, and nearly every person has some particular weakness that upsets him. For example, I know people who can endure prolonged physical suffering but will go to pieces at the slightest criticism. One of my vulnerable characteristics is impatience. I have friends who can fish all day in one spot and have a perfectly marvelous time whether they catch anything or not. I cannot do that. I actually believe I was born in a hurry, so that when things go slowly I get irritated. I have recognized that weakness and have made a lot of progress. One afternoon I was driving out of downtown Atlanta about 5:30 in the afternoon. The traffic was heavy and slow, and I had to creep along. I was beginning to get upset, and then I caught myself. I thought about how long it would take me to drive from where I was to my home if there were no traffic at all. I decided it would take ten minutes. Then I looked at my watch and decided to find out, just for fun, how long it would take in that heavy traffic. Then I just relaxed, turned on the radio, and settled down. It took me exactly sixteen minutes to get home. Just six minutes more. I was thoroughly

ashamed of myself. There I was about to get upset over six minutes. I decided that my time is not that valuable.

Study yourself. What are the things that irritate and upset you? I dare say that in most instances they are simply not worth bothering about at all. So study to strengthen yourself where you are emotionally weak.

2. *Study people.* The study of people is the most interesting study in the world; so, instead of letting some person upset you, study him objectively. For example, suppose a store clerk is rude to you. Instead of getting angry and making a fool of yourself, start asking yourself why the clerk is rude. Perhaps a previous customer had upset him, and he was taking it out on you. A member of his family may be very sick, and he is worried. Perhaps he has a toothache, or is worried over a debt and doesn't know how he can pay it. If you knew all the facts, you probably would feel sorry for him instead of being angry with him. Instead of letting people upset you, get interested in them and you will learn a lot and maintain your own self-control at the same time.

3. *Study the price you pay for getting upset.* You may have to pay a doctor and a medical bill. You may even have to go to a hospital. A physician told me recently that fully half of his patients were sick because of emotional disturbances. When you become sick you lose time from your work and cannot do a lot of things that you would do if you were well.

Or your emotional uncontrol may destroy your home. Nothing in life is more precious than the love of a wife or a husband. But if you keep on "flying off the handle," saying things you do not mean, pouting and nagging and acting like a spoiled brat, that love can be killed. To lose the peace and joy of your home is a mighty high price to pay.

You cannot do your work nearly so well when you get angry and lose your self-control. Thus you drive away customers, or cheat yourself out of a promotion. You are forced to swallow the bitter pill of seeing your fellow workers get ahead of you.

4. *Recognize the presence of God.* I used to play golf with a man who was addicted to profanity. Yet, because I was a minister, he never uttered an oath in my presence. When I was with him he controlled himself. Now, if he fully realized that at all times and in all places he was in the presence of Almighty God, he would never utter another oath.

Mrs. Fulton Oursler says that she used to count to ten when she found herself getting upset, but it did not help much. Then one day she noticed the first ten words of the Lord's Prayer. So now, instead of counting to ten she says over and over, "Our Father which art in heaven, hallowed be thy name." When one's mind becomes saturated with those ten words, their influence is magical. Remember that the prophet Isaiah said, "In quietness and in confidence shall be your strength" (Isaiah 30:15). To become strong, learn to control your emotions.

## Three Difficulties in Living Today

1. One of the difficulties in living today is that we are burdened by our old decisions of yesterday. Where is there one among us who has not said, "If I had only made a different decision, my life would be better now"? Suppose you had married some other person, or entered some other line of work, or settled in some other city? One help at this point is to remind yourself that you do not know the road you did not take. In your imagination you think of that other road as being smooth and straight and leading directly to your heart's desire, but in reality you cannot be sure. That other road may have been more wearisome and more heartbreaking. A second help is to remind yourself that you have not yet seen all of the road which you did choose. Maybe you are having hardships and difficulties now, but who knows?—tomorrow may bring a turning point. If not tomorrow, maybe next week, or next month, or next year. It is just possible that on the road you are now traveling, you will run head-on into happiness—the happiness you had begun to think was on the road you did not choose.

One day, the British prime minister David Lloyd George and a friend of his were walking across a field. As they walked, Lloyd's friend asked him how he had been able to keep his inner composure and strength during the difficult days of the First World War. As they came to the end of the field, Mr. George opened the gate, and after they had walked through, he carefully closed it. Then he said, "Right here is my secret. I always close the gate behind me and concentrate on where I am walking now." In order to be able to give our best to the present, we must be able to close the gates of the past.

2. We must realize that many of the hardships and unhappiness of today are not permanent. Someone once asked an old retired minister what his favorite Bible verse was. Quickly came his reply: "And it came to pass." He went on to explain that through a long life he had come to realize that the heartaches, troubles, wars,

debts, and all of the burdens of mankind will eventually "come to pass." One remembers the words spoken to Job: "Thou shalt forget thy misery, and remember it as waters that pass away" (Job 11:16).

This same truth applies to the happy, delightful experiences of life as well. We need to learn to enjoy the joys of each day, because they, too, "come to pass." They shouldn't be wasted, because they only last a short while. Wouldn't it be wonderful if we could keep that precious little child in our home, just as he is, so that one day, when we had time, we could play with him and enjoy him? But that little child doesn't stay the way he is. He will grow up, and if we expect to enjoy that child, we have to enjoy him when we have the opportunity.

So, in both our burdens and our pleasures, let us remember that they "come to pass." Knowing this truth, we can face life squarely day by day.

3. In living one day at a time, we must not try to run ahead into tomorrow. Isn't it true that most of our worries are borrowed from tomorrow? We worry about mountains we may never have to climb, about streams we may never have to cross, about enemies we may never have to face. It has been pointed out that Lloyd's of London has gotten rich by betting that what people worry about will never happen.

Thomas S. Kepler tells about a group of 104 psychologists who made a study of their cases and determined a timetable for anxiety: At eighteen, we worry about ideals; at twenty, we worry about appearance; at twenty-three, about morals; at twenty-six, about making a good impression; at thirty, about salary and the cost of living; at thirty-one, about business success; at thirty-three, about job security; at forty-one, about loss of ambition; over forty-five, about health. Most of these worries are useless.

One assurance that helps us to overcome our fears for tomorrow is the fact that we will be given the strength we need. We are promised in God's Word: "As thy days, so shall thy strength be" (Deuteronomy 33:25); that is, we will have the strength we need when the time comes. Professor MacDougall has told the story about a boy who was chased across a field by an infuriated bull. He succeeded in leaping over a high fence and saving himself. Some time later, the boy went back to that fence and tried to jump it again. He made repeated efforts, but never could accomplish it; yet in his moment of great need he had had unusual strength and was able to jump it.

What we often do is anticipate our needs in the future and try to match them with our present resources. We fail to consider that perhaps we will be stronger and more able to meet our needs when those needs arise. You are stronger than you think. You are braver than you think. Wait until the need arises before you begin to worry about it. Just concentrate on the living of today. As one puts his best into the living of each day, he goes a long way toward the elimination of his worries, fears, and anxieties about the future.

## Handle Your Disappointments

Disappointments come to all of us, and the more I see of life, the more convinced I am that one of the most important lessons any person can learn is how to handle a disappointment. One of the bitterest disappointments I ever had was when I was in grammar school. We were having a Christmas party and each student had drawn at random the name of some other student for whom he was to bring a present. Each of us brought his present that day, and finally time came to give them out. The teacher took the presents off the tree and called out the names. Each time I hoped that the next present would be mine, but finally she called the last present and never did call my name. I was the only one in that class who went home without a present. What had happened was that the one who had drawn my name was sick and could not come that day. But I learned early in life that a disappointment can be a hard experience.

I know mothers and fathers who are disappointed in their children. Many are disappointed because of lack of career opportunities. One of the loveliest young ladies I know came and told me that the boy she expected to marry had written her that he had decided to marry another girl. Disappointments have broken a lot of hearts. I am even sympathetic with the little boy who slipped under the side of a big tent, thinking it was a circus. After he got in he discovered it was a revival meeting. I know how he felt!

A disappointment causes a bad mental wound. It cuts deeply and hurts terribly. And, if one is not careful, the wound that disappointment makes can become infected. Bitterness can get started there. Anger, hatred, jealousy, worry, and fear thrive on disappointments. Disappointment can give a good start in our minds to things such as despair, hopelessness, and a "what's-the-use?" spirit.

But there is a helpful prescription that I frequently give to people. If faithfully taken, it is a sure cure. Here it is: "Delight thyself also in the Lord; and he shall give thee the desires of thine heart. Commit thy way unto the Lord; trust also in him; and he shall bring it to pass" (Psalms 37:4, 5).

Notice some of the elements in that prescription. "Commit thy way unto the Lord." There is glorious peace and power in doing the best that you can and then trusting in God, believing that somehow things will work out for the best.

One of the most clever and helpful sayings that I have ever heard came from a man who told me, "I have changed my *dis*appointments to '*His* appointments.' " Whatever happens, this man believes that God knows all about it, and so he just accepts it and goes on.

Who is wise enough to plot his own future? We cannot understand a lot of things right here in the present. Why do we make the enormous assumption that we have the wisdom to plot our future? It is hard to see God's hand in many things that happen; you may not understand today why it happened that way. It may take a year or maybe even twenty years, but, if you keep your faith, you will eventually see that things do happen for the best. God will "give thee the desires of thine heart." So, in the meantime, "delight thyself also in the Lord." Don't get sour and bitter. Keep a smile on your face, keep "singing in the rain," and, above all, keep going. Remember, "He shall bring it to pass."

I stood recently on a bridge over the great Mississippi River. I thought of William Alexander Percy's little book *Lanterns on the Levee*, which tells about how men would patrol the levees when the big river was at flood stage. At night the wives of these men could look out and see the lanterns and feel safe, knowing they were being watched over. Then I looked at that Mississippi delta land and I thought of how time and again that land has been flooded, bringing disappointment to a lot of people. Houses are wrecked and crops are destroyed. But each flood leaves a deposit of soil, and today that land is one of the richest sections of farmland in all the world. The flood of disappointment hurts, but it leaves life richer and better when it is borne with endurance.

## When Life Seems Too Crowded

Every so often I get up in the morning saying, "I just cannot do all the things I feel I must do today." Sometimes when I am in such a mood, I feel confused and don't know where to begin. It is then that I take three steps which I have found to be of great help:

1. *Make a list.* First, I take pencil and paper and make a list of the

things I need to do this day. Then I arrange the list in the order I want to take up each task, estimating how much time each will take. Often I find I can do everything on my list and even have an hour or two to spare. Sometimes I find there is too much to do, so I strike off some of the items that can be put off.

After making my list of things to do, I stop thinking of everything on the list except the first item. When that is finished, I take up the second item, and continue that way on down the list. It is amazing how much easier it works out and how much calmer and clearer my mind is when following this procedure. It is like the old proverb which says, "The longest journey begins with a single step." Instead of thinking of the long journey, think of the next step and complete it.

It has been well said:

> God broke the years to hours and days,
>    That hour by hour and day by day,
> Just going on a little way,
>    We might be able all along
> To keep our spirit poised and strong.

By taking one step at a time, you can walk a long way in a day. And by giving yourself to one task at a time, you can accomplish more than you ever thought you could. If you are a housewife, you cannot wash the dishes, sweep the floor, and make the beds all at the same time. Just put your mind on one task and do that, and then turn to the next. If you are an office manager, you can make one decision at a time, refusing to worry about the next decision until the first one is settled. If you are a secretary, you can type only one letter at a time. We squander our power when we try to do one job while carrying the load of another job on our minds at the same time.

2. Next, just as you must concentrate on the one task at hand, also *concentrate on living this one day*. Too often we add to this day the burdens of yesterday and tomorrow. It is so easy, and so disintegrating, to review and regret old decisions. Instead, we should profit from our mistakes by learning from them; but we should stop worrying about them.

Take, for example, the two most important decisions of your life, next to your decision for Christ: (1) your choice of a life's work, and (2) your selection of a mate. Have you wondered if you might not have gone further and been happier if you had taken another road, or married another person? Add to those two questions a multitude of other wonderings about whether you did the right thing, and very quickly life becomes a very heavy burden, indeed. However, in most cases it is too late to go back and start over again. We need to get on with living life today. Futile regrets over yesterday and appreciation over tomorrow will get you nowhere.

Paul learned the secret: ". . . this one thing I do, forgetting those things which are behind . . ." (Philippians 3:13). The Revised Standard Version of the Bible makes Jesus' words clearer: "Let the day's own trouble be sufficient for the day" (Matthew 6:34 RSV). There you have it—tackle one job at a time and live one day at a time.

3. *Always remember that you are stronger than you think.* I doubt if any person has ever used all his strength. God made the human body with adrenaline glands which secrete and supply energy when it is needed for an emergency. I know of a farmer who was sitting on his porch one day watching his son drive toward the house in a pickup truck. Something went wrong and the truck ran into a ditch and turned over, pinning the boy underneath. The father ran to the place, lifted the truck, and pulled the boy out from under it. Later he tried to lift that truck again but he could not budge it. The emergency had brought forth strength to meet it.

Every mother understands this. One night she goes to bed so tired that she feels she could not walk across the room one more time if her life depended on it. But if one of her children suddenly becomes ill and cries out, immediately the mother is on her feet and ready to watch over and minister to that child throughout the remainder of the night. She had strength she had not known before.

I believe this is what is meant in the Bible passage that says, ". . . and as thy days, so shall thy strength be" (Deuteronomy 33:25). We will have the strength to do what each day calls for—the heavier and harder the day, the greater our strength will be to face it. Remember Psalms 23:5: "Thou preparest a table before me in the presence of mine enemies." In other words, in the midst of our needs, God supplies the resources.

Not only did God make our bodies with reserve strength, but also He made our spirits with reserve strength. Sometimes we feel like saying, "I cannot go through this," but when the time comes we usually find that we can. We can stand far more than we realize. I like the title of a minister-friend's sermon: "You Are Braver Than You Think"—and you are. The chances are that when the time comes, you are more likely to stand up with courage than you are to become a coward.

Not only do you have reserve strengths which rise to your aid when the need comes, but more important is the power and grace of Almighty God. Someone asked D. L. Moody if he had "dying grace." He answered, "No, I have living grace, but when the times comes that I need it, God will then give me 'dying grace.' " And we recall how Paul prayed again and again that the "thorn in his flesh" be removed; instead, God gave him the grace to bear it. God supplies the added strength that you need, if you ask Him for it and have faith.

## When You Are Blocked

As the children of Israel journeyed toward the realization of their dreams, the possession of their Promised Land, the word came that Pharaoh had changed his mind about letting them go free. The hated dictator was now after them with his armies. They hurried their pace; they broke camp earlier and marched longer into the night, hoping they could keep ahead of Pharaoh.

Then came that dreadful day when they came to the Red Sea. There it stretched before them to block their path. They had no boats; they could go no farther; they had no weapons to fight the army behind them. There was no hope either forward or backward. Their only course was helpless surrender.

Now comes one of the grandest scenes in the entire Bible. I am not referring to the dividing of the Red Sea. To see the waters roll back and the dry land appear, providing a pathway to safety, was wonderful, but that was really the anticlimax. Even more wonderful was what happened before. In the midst of their anguished disappointment, Moses stood up and got the attention of his people. Notice what he said: "Fear ye not, stand still, and see the salvation of the Lord, which he will show to you today. . . . The Lord shall fight for you, and ye shall hold your peace" (Exodus 14:13, 14).

What a marvelous faith he had! The Israelites had been so busy and hurried that they had forgotten that God could help them. "Stand still," Moses said. We remember how the psalmist said, "Be still, and know that I am God" (Psalms 46:10). One of our greatest needs is to learn how to quiet our spirits, to still our minds, and give God a chance with us. As we realize God's presence, the anxieties of life lose their hold upon us. Annie Johnson Flint wrote this poem about God's leading presence:

> Have you come to the Red Sea place in your life,
>   Where in spite of all you can do
> There is no way out, there is no way back,
>   There is no other way but through?
> Then wait on the Lord with a trust serene,
>   Till the night of your fear is gone.
> He will send the winds, He will heap the floods,
>   When He says to your soul "Go on."
>
> And His hand will lead you through, clear through.
>   Ere the watery walls roll down,
> No wave can touch you, no foe can smite,
>   No mightiest sea can drown.
> The tossing billows may rear their crests,
>   Their foam at your feet may break,
> But over their bed you shall walk dry shod,
>   In the path that your Lord shall make.
>
> In the morning watch, 'neath the lifted clouds,
>   You shall see but the Lord alone,
> When He leads you forth from the place of the sea,
>   To a land that you have not known.
> And your fears shall pass as your foes shall pass.
>   You shall be no more afraid.
> You shall sing His praise in a better place,
>   In a place that His hands hath made.

## Quiet Your Mind

In a very difficult moment, when it seemed that all was lost, Moses said words to his people that we also need to hear: "Stand still, and see the salvation of the Lord. . . ." In times of anxious fear, our greatest need is to quiet our minds.

A church where I formerly served as pastor had a beautiful series of twenty-three stained-glass windows depicting the life of our Lord. These windows were created by one of the oldest stained-glass companies in the world. For more than three hundred years this company has studied ways to create windows that will develop a mood of worship in the minds of the people. The one climactic scene of these windows is the one behind the pulpit, directly in front of the people during the service. It shows the ascension of Christ. More than half of the window is deep-blue sky. Some have said there was too much blue in it, but the artist knew what he was doing when he made it that way. Psychological studies have shown that the color blue reduces tension, blood pressure, and heart action, and relieves anxiety. Blue creates an atmosphere in which one can more easily throw off the worries of daily life and let the Spirit of God into his mind.

A friend of mine once talked with the man who repairs the windows in the Cathedral of Chartres in France. This man said that the one color which has not disintegrated under the elements during the centuries is the blue used by the ancient craftsmen. He declared that one reason Chartres is so stimulating to the human spirit is because of the deep blues through which the light filters.

The main point is this: if the color through which we look at the light influences our minds and spirits, how much greater are we influenced by the windows through which we look at life. Moses said, "Stand still, and see the salvation of the Lord. . . ." That is, first get God in your mind and then look at your problems through the window of your faith. Color your thinking with God and your anxieties will cease to dominate you.

Be still right now for one minute. Let your body relax. Think of God as being right at your side; think of His power flowing into you. Think of Him opening the way through some problem of your life. Feel deep peace possessing your mind. "The Lord shall fight for you and ye shall hold your peace." Amen.

## What's Your Hurry?

The minister met me at the plane and said, "We don't have time to wait for your baggage. Someone else will get it. You are to speak at the club in twenty minutes." As we hurried from the airport into town, he told me the schedule for the week. Each morning at nine o'clock there was to be a talk on television and at ten o'clock a church service; then each night another service at the church. There were to be three civic club talks, talks at two high schools, and one talk to the women's club. It all added up to nineteen speaking engagements in four-and-a-half days. In addition, certain hours had been scheduled for personal counseling.

I got along fairly well until Wednesday night. I went to bed that night but I couldn't get to sleep. I read a magazine, I walked about the room, I took a warm shower, but nothing helped. I have some little mental tricks I sometimes use to get off to sleep, but they all failed. I had let myself get wound up too tightly. Finally I did get a little restless sleep, but the next morning I felt terrible.

After the ten o'clock service, I told the pastor I would be gone for the remainder of the day. I started walking slowly down the street, going no place in particular and in no hurry to get there. A number of people spoke to me and stopped and talked awhile. It reminded me of living in a little town where you can enjoy visiting up and down Main Street.

I walked on past the city limits until I came to the big bridge on the river. I found a comfortable place to sit down and I sat there for two hours watching the river. I thought of Grove Patterson's experience: while sitting on a bridge watching the water flow, he thought of the expression, "under the bridge." Our troubles and hardships eventually go "under the bridge" of the present moment and pass by.

From the bridge I could see the point where two rivers flowed together. One of the rivers was almost clear, the other extremely muddy. For a short distance after they came together, you could distinguish the water of each, but a little farther on the clear water took on the brownish color of the other. I thought about how we let evil thoughts come into our minds and how the evil soon colors all our living. I made some mental notes for a sermon about that.

At the end of the bridge was a tiny hamburger place. I ordered a burger with onions; in fact, I asked for an *extra* onion. It tasted real good and I didn't care whether or not it left an odor on my breath. I had been so pious all week that I was in the mood to do something daring! Eating onions made me feel independent.

I walked on along the road until I came to a cemetery. It reminded me of a prescription a physician once gave his patient: spend an hour a day for a week walking in the cemetery, and remember that the people there thought they had to do everything, but now the world is going along fine without them.

"Barge-itis" is one of the worst of our modern diseases. So many people rush around and rudely barge in ahead of others. Watch the cars waiting for a red light. At the first flicker of the light changing, many drivers stomp down on the accelerator and "peel out." If a car ahead hesitates for even a second, they impatiently blow the horn. I even notice signs of "barge-itis" at church. Some people sit on the edge of the pew and never really settle down. If the service runs a minute overtime, they impatiently look at their watches. When the benediction is announced, they make a mad dash toward the door. I sometimes want to stand at the door and ask, "What's your hurry?" Most would have no answer because they really have nothing to hurry them; they are just afflicted with "barge-itis."

I spent an hour walking among the graves. During that hour I was the only person there. I thought about how quickly someone is forgotten and how others take our places. It is not so important that we carry the world on our shoulders as we sometimes think.

I got back to the hotel in time for dinner before the preaching service that night. I felt rested and relaxed. When I got back to my room after the service, I went to bed. I picked up my Bible from the table and opened it to the Thirty-seventh Psalm. Next to the Twenty-third, that is my favorite psalm. It was written for people who get disturbed and overwrought. The Thirty-seventh Psalm is gentle and tender, like a sweet, kindly mother putting her hand upon the brow of a restless child. The psalm begins, "Fret not thyself. . . ." It goes on to say, "Delight thyself also in the Lord; and he shall give thee the desires of thine heart" (verse 4). Further on we read, "Rest in the Lord, and wait patiently for him . . ." (verse 7). All the way through, the psalm leads one to a calm and a triumphant faith. That night I slept easily and the next day I felt rested and strong.

Many times I have listened to the motors of a giant airliner. As the plane roars down the runway for the takeoff, it uses all of its power to lift itself off the ground and into the air. But very quickly after takeoff you can tell that the pilot has eased back the throttles; the big plane climbs into the air and finally levels off. Then the big motors are throttled down still more. The pilot will tell you, "If I run the engines at full power too long, it will harm them." So it is with each of us. There are times when we must go at our full power. But if one does not learn to ease back the throttle, level off, and hit a steady cruising speed, eventually he will become torn asunder by strain and stress—especially that which we put on our minds.

I know a man who is confined to a wheelchair, yet he is burning himself out. His mind is constantly rushing to this and that. He worries about his business; he has an uneasy conscience which tortures him; he is filled with unrest and tension. He has never learned to level off.

## "Fear Not!"

When we encounter sickness, the loss of a job, the death of a loved one, bankruptcy, or an endless number of other tragedies, we feel defeated. We make various responses to seeming defeat. I say *seeming* because I do not believe that defeat is ever final. It is a momentary situation and there is always another chapter yet to be written. But at the moment such a circumstance occurs, our response very likely is *fear*.

It is a strange coincidence that the Bible repeats the command "Fear not" exactly 365 times—once for each day of the year! It is as if to say that there is no day in our lives when fear is not a present reality. When things are going fairly well, we tend to deny the presence of fear. On the other hand, when we recognize the presence of faith, we no longer need to deny fear. When we have faith, we can assure ourselves that it is perfectly all right to be afraid. Being fearful is not unchristian and neither is it a sign of weakness. Recognizing fear is a sign of faith, as well as courage and confidence. You will have come a long way in life when you reach the point at which you care to face fear, because then you are ready to cope with it. Here are three steps for dealing with fear:

1. *Admit it.* Maybe you do not need to shout it from the housetops, but at least in your own heart face up to the fact that you are afraid. The very recognition of fear is a victory within itself. It is a strong step toward self-confidence.

2. *Accept it.* If you are sick, and lurking in the darkness is the fear of "sickness unto death," you might tell yourself that the doctor has made a mistake—that it cannot be true. You can do the same with your fears. But many things you fear are true. Some things are not going to be changed; and we must learn to live with them. Acceptance is never easy and it may be painful. But it is also freeing. We reach the point that we do not have to pretend any more, not even to ourselves. We do not have to feel that we are failures, or that we are weak, or that we are different from other people. We can escape that feeling that somehow we are guilty, and we can stop running and trying to hide. When we accept our fears, we are ready for the third step.

3. *Do something about it.* Start with identifying what your fears are. A good point to remember is that nearly all the fears that any person has have been learned; they are not natural, with the exception of just two. Many people believe that the two natural, unlearned fears are the fear of falling and the fear of a sudden loud noise. Every other fear is one that we have picked up somewhere along the way. These fears include: being alone, riding in an airplane, facing old age, losing your material possessions, fire, getting stuck on an elevator, the sight of blood, going to the

dentist, losing your mind, talking to the boss, cancer, a heart attack, the end of the world—and to these fears each of us can add many others.

Instead of worrying about how to get rid of all your fears, emphasize your faith to the point that you are willing to accept your fears and face up to them. In fact, we can go even further and make friends with our fears. What I mean is that we should recognize the fact that fear can be constructive and positive and important in every human life. Fear is not necessarily an enemy and we need not worry about how to get rid of our fears. The truth is, fear is a God-given emotion for our protection and for our own good. There are many things that we *should* fear. I have heard it said, "If you don't draw us by love, you can never drive us by fear." That simply is not the truth. We do many things because we are afraid not to do them: we obey the speed limit; we pay our income taxes; we visit the doctor. Fear causes us to seek further knowledge. If man did not fear cancer, then all of the research carried on to prevent it would never have been done. Once we recognize the fear, then we seek to learn how to cope with it. Without fear there would be no faith. Fear is a stimulation to the very highest living.

Let us be very clear at this point—fear is not failure—fear is not weakness—fear need not be destructive—we do not need to be ashamed of our fears—fear stimulates faith—fear is the inspiration to endeavor—fear is the doorway to wisdom. Therefore, we do not need to fear fear.

I like the words of Scottish poet Joanna Baillie:

> *The brave man is not he who feels no fear,*
> *For that were stupid and irrational;*
> *But he, whose noble soul its fears subdues*
> *And bravely dares the danger nature shrinks from.*

There are two things which we should not fear. One of them is that which we *can* change. If we can do something about it, let us stop wringing our hands in useless fear. Let's get to work to do something about it. The second thing we should not fear is that which we *cannot* change. If there is nothing we can do about it, then, to put it simply, there is nothing we can do about it. One of the most prayed prayers in all the world is the prayer that Professor Reinhold Niebuhr wrote many years ago:

*God grant me the serenity*
*To accept the things I cannot change;*
*The courage to change the things I can,*
*And the wisdom to know the difference.*

Here is a good place to summarize a very fundamental principle in reference to fear. As I've said before, live one day at a time. You can't relive the past and you can't live the future. There is no need to hold on to the failures of yesterday nor to manufacture fears for tomorrow. Do the best you can right now in spite of what has happened in the past. I know this has been said over and over again, but I also know that we need to keep saying it—and *doing* it.

Sir William Osler, the distinguished physician, once said, "The load of tomorrow, added to that of yesterday, carried today, makes the strongest falter." He went on to say, "we should live in date-tight compartments, not letting yesterday and tomorrow intrude on our lives." He concluded, "Then, you will avoid the waste of energy, the mental distress, the nervous worries that dog the steps of the man who is anxious about the future."

Or as Honoré de Balzac, the nineteenth-century French author, put it: "After all, our worst misfortunes never happen and most miseries lie in anticipation."

## Do Something for Somebody

Another thing that needs to be said about fear is that it can be dealt with if we stop thinking about ourselves and start doing something for somebody else. If you feel a fear coming on, think of somebody who is lonely, or worried, or who needs help. Buy that person a card or a present, and take it or send it to that person. It is marvelous what that simple little act of kindness to someone will do for you. Oftentimes it can do as much for you as a visit to a psychiatrist, and it is a lot less expensive!

Edward Everett Hale said something worth repeating:

*To look up and not down,*
*To look forward and not back,*
*To look out and not in, and*
*To lend a hand.*

I especially emphasize that last phrase "and to lend a hand." George Bernard Shaw described a certain person as "a selfish little clod of ailments and grievances, complaining that the world will not devote itself to making [him] happy." Unselfish service to others can turn even the utmost tragedy into victory. Let us well remember this truth—happy people are helpful people.

## Trust in God

When fear is before us, let us trust in God. This does not mean that God provides us an escape from all the troubles of life, but we do have the promise of His fellowship and companionship. I am not a fatalist, but I believe that nothing will ever happen that God does not permit to happen. Therefore, we need to trust God's will and guidance. The great psychologist Carl Jung once said, "The greatest and most important problems of life can never be solved, but only outgrown."

Once I saw a little poster in the lobby of a hospital that read: "Worrying is like a rocking chair. It will give you something to do, but will get you nowhere." That is not true with fear. Fear will accomplish things. Fear is one of life's driving forces to help mankind reach the highest heights.

I think Van Dyke says it best in "The Voyagers":

> O Maker of the Mighty Deep,
>   Whereon our vessels fare,
> Above our life's adventure keep
>   Thy faithful watch and care.
> In Thee we trust, whate'er befall;
> Thy sea is great, our boats are small.
>
> We know not where the secret tides
>   Will help us or delay,
> Nor where the lurking tempest hides
>   Nor where the fogs are gray.
> We trust in Thee, whate'er befall;
> Thy sea is great, our boats are small. . . .

We can deal with defeat without getting desperate, even though our boats are small, when we recognize that defeat is not final. There was a time when Demosthenes, the great Greek orator, could no longer hide from the people the fact that he stuttered. Finally, he took it into the world, where people could see it, and only then could he begin to conquer his stuttering tongue. Charles Steinmetz, the great scientist, came to believe that he could be a useful person in spite of the fact that his body was terribly deformed. Milton was blind, but eventually he believed that, despite his blindness, he could write poetry that could make life sing. Robert Louis Stevenson suffered physical pain all of the time, but during his sickest years, he wrote some of his greatest masterpieces. Beethoven could give to the world a composition like the Ninth Symphony even though he was deaf and could not hear it himself. Louis Pasteur made his greatest contribution after he had a stroke. We do react to certain situations with fear, but we also use fear as a springboard.

# 7

## *The Seventh Spiritual Wonder:*

# Your Own Christian Experience

 "How can I be born again?" That is a question that has been on the lips of countless people. We know Jesus said, "Ye must be born again" (John 3:7). We have heard preachers talk about born again people. However, this has caused confusion in the minds of many people. No one can really explain the "new birth." There are other terms that are used synonymously, such as, "the Christian experience," "being saved," and many others. The important thing to remember is that this most important experience in life comes in different ways. Some people tend to feel that everybody must have the identical experience. There are those who feel disturbed because they have not had the experience they hear someone tell about. Let us look at three very common types of new birth experiences in the Bible.

The first example is in the ninth chapter of the Book of Acts. There we read the story of the most dramatic, climactic Christian experience we can find. Saul of Tarsus was on the road to Damascus. Suddenly, he saw a bright light from heaven shining all around him. "He fell to the earth, and heard a voice saying unto him, Saul, Saul, why persecutest thou me?" (verse 4). He responded to that call and became a Christian, and in becoming a Christian, his name was changed from Saul to Paul. As long as he lived, Paul could say, "A certain day at a certain place, I became a Christian."

There is a little song that goes like this:

*I can tell you now the time,*
*I can take you to the place:*
*Where the Lord saved me,*
*By His wonderful grace.*

Many people can sing that song. It might have happened in a particular church service or in one of many other places, but they know the exact moment and the circumstance. It was a dramatic, overwhelming, glorious experience. However, that is not the only type of new birth. In fact, many of us do not believe it is the best type.

As an old man in prison, Paul wrote to Timothy, his dearly beloved friend. Paul probably loved Timothy more than he loved any other person on the earth at that time, and he expected Timothy to carry on his work. He wrote to Timothy, "From a child thou hast known the holy scriptures, which are able to make thee wise unto salvation . . ." (2 Timothy 3:15). He writes to Timothy, "When I call to remembrance the unfeigned faith that is in thee, which dwelt first in thy grandmother Lois, and thy mother Eunice; and I am persuaded that in thee also" (2 Timothy 1:5). He is saying to Timothy that his grandmother was a Christian and his mother was a Christian and that he grew up believing himself to be a Christian and never knowing himself to be anything else.

There has been a great change in the methods of many of our churches. In the churches in which I grew up, not much attention was paid to the children and the young people. In the summer they would have a revival. Every effort was made to stir up the emotions and high pressure people to "'walk down the aisle" and express their faith. Today churches give a lot more attention to children. They are trained and nurtured before they can walk, and they are taught the Bible and the fact that God loves them, and they grow up believing themselves to be Christians and never knowing themselves to be anything else.

Many of us were prayed for before we were born. The first song we ever learned to sing was, "Jesus loves me! this I know." Before we can remember, we were taught each night to kneel at our bedsides and pray, "Now I lay me down to sleep. . . ." When we went to the table for a meal, it was the normal and natural thing to bow our heads and have a prayer thanking God for His goodness. We were raised as Christians in Christian homes. We never hated God; we never went with the Prodigal Son to the "far country."

We do know Jesus said we must be born again, but we also know that new birth can come so normally and so naturally that we never know the exact moment that it came. We cannot name a certain time and place, yet we are just as certain that it has happened to us.

The third type of new birth experience is in the nineteenth chapter of Luke's Gospel. Jesus came to the city of Jericho. Living there was a man by the name of Zaccheus. Zaccheus was both prominent and wealthy in that city, but he was also short in height. He wanted to see Jesus, but so many people lined the road that he could not see over them. So Zaccheus climbed up into a sycamore tree to see Jesus as He went by. Then we read, "And when Jesus came to the place, he looked up, and saw him, and said unto him, Zaccheus, make haste, and come down; for today I must abide at thy house. And he made haste, and came down, and received him joyfully" (Luke 19:5, 6).

We see them going to Zaccheus's home together. The curtain comes down, and you do not see them for a time, maybe two or three hours. Then the curtain comes up and you hear Jesus say, "This day is salvation come to this house . . ." (Luke 19:9). Jesus is saying to Zaccheus that he has been saved—that he has had a Christian experience—that he has been born again.

Let us ask ourselves what happened. My answer would be that they sat quietly together in Zaccheus's home. As Zaccheus talked with Jesus, he saw that the life of Jesus was so much better than his own life that, no matter what it cost him, he would pay the price and make a commitment to Christ. I do not think he shouted about it; I doubt if he even cried. I imagine it was just a quiet, simple decision that took place there in that room. Many people have had quiet births in Christ, in many different places, and that experience is just as real.

The important thing is not the how but the fact of the new birth, which may take place in different ways. When one receives the new birth, there are four important things that happen:

1. A liberating sense of forgiveness comes into one's soul. It means not so much that our sins have been taken away, but that a relationship with God has been consummated. There comes a certain feeling of, as the song says, "nothing between my soul and the Saviour." We feel free.

2. In the new birth experience, there comes a new sense of power. We feel power over temptation; we feel the power to do what we formerly thought was impossible. We especially realize that God has power in His world. The last words of the Lord's

Prayer take on new meaning to us: "For thine is the kingdom, and the power, and the glory, for ever. Amen" (Matthew 6:13).

3. When the Spirit of God has come into our hearts, we feel a sense of peace. It brings to us quiet hearts born of clear consciences and a sense of adequacy. No verse in the Bible describes this feeling better than these words: "Peace I leave with you, my peace I give unto you: not as the world giveth, give I unto you. Let not your heart be troubled, neither let it be afraid" (John 14:27).

4. Out of the experience of Christ in our hearts there comes an outgoing love for other people. When we are born we naturally love our mother and our father. We come to love our brothers and sisters and our families, and we come to love our friends. But when Christ comes into our hearts, then we come to love everybody.

## You Know Enough to Be Saved

Many ministers and church-school teachers have had the experience of leading some child to a decision for Christ, and then had the parents object to the child's joining the church on the ground that they do not know enough about it. That same objection also has kept many adults out of the church who otherwise would have joined. Thus I ask the question, "What must I know to be saved?"

One of the most genuine and challenging conversions on record is the case of the Philippian jailer. The validity of his experience can hardly be questioned, and yet he was no theologian. He was a heathen who knew next to nothing about Christ. It is probable that he never saw the Scriptures of his day. And if he had seen them, he most likely could not have read them. Paul and Silas may have been the only Christians he ever talked to. It is almost certain that he was never inside a Christian church. And certainly he did not have the advantages of a church school, with all its wonderful teachings and inspiration. And, more important still, he had no Christian parents to live the good life before him from babyhood and to throw about him the influences of a Christian home. Nevertheless, he would be a fit candidate for membership in any church.

One does not have to wait until he knows and understands all about Christ to be saved. None of us really understands electricity. Lord Kelvin, the foremost physicist of his day, declared, "If I were asked what electricity is, actually is, I should have to confess I know nothing about it." But while I do not know all about electricity, I am not going to sit in the dark until I do. I know two things about it: I know I need light and that electricity supplies that need. That is enough to begin on. I do not know all about digestion, how food turns into blood and bone and tissue, but I'm not going to sit and starve until I do know. I know that food will satisfy my hunger and give me strength, and that is enough to begin on. I do not understand all about Christ. It is something of a mystery to me how Christ actually saves a soul and a life. I have never seen anyone who could fully explain it. Yet I do know that when I completely dedicate my life to Him, He meets my deepest need, and right then salvation is mine. That is enough to know to begin on.

While a law student at Yale, Horace Bushnell was an unbeliever. During a great revival that was sweeping the university, his conscience began to bother him because he realized that many undergraduates refused to attend the revival meeting because he had urged them not to attend. One day he faced the question, "If I do not believe in Christ, what do I believe in?" He decided that there was an absolute difference between right and wrong. His next question was, "Have I put myself on the side of right, to follow it regardless of consequence?" He answered, "I have not, but I will," and then and there he dedicated himself to the principle of right. The result was that after he had been a minister in Hartford, Connecticut, for forty-seven years, he said, "Better than I know any man in Hartford, I know Jesus Christ."

Dr. Charles F. Banning relates an experience of Dr. John B. Gough. While a guest in a home, he was asked by the mother to talk with her boy. Upstairs in his room the great reformer found a miserable, degraded piece of humanity. "Edward," said he, "do you not sometimes regret terribly the life you are leading?"

"Indeed I do, Mr. Gough."

"Then why do you not abandon it?"

"I cannot," came the answer. "I am bound hand and foot, and I will have to go on this way until I die."

"Edward, do you ever pray?"

"No. I do not believe in God. I do not believe in anything."

"Edward, do you believe in your mother?"

"Yes, Mr. Gough, that is the only thing in the world that I do believe in."

"Edward, do you think your mother loves you?"

"Oh, I am sure of it."

"Then you believe in love, don't you? You believe that there is at least one good thing in the world, and that is love, because your mother loves you."

"Well, yes, I suppose I do believe in love."

"Edward, when I have gone out," pleaded Mr. Gough, "will you promise me that you will kneel down and offer a prayer to love, and ask love to help you?"

The boy hesitated, but promised. After Mr. Gough had gone, feeling (as he said afterward) like a fool, the boy prayed. "O Love," he said, and instantly came a voice to his soul, saying, "God is love." Then he cried, "O God." There came back to him a verse which his mother had taught him, "For God so loved the world, that he gave his only begotten Son." Then the boy shouted, "O Christ," and the heavens opened and into his life came a flood of forgiveness and joy, and he rushed down the stairs to his mother to tell her that he had found the Christ.

I was five years old when I went forward on the invitation to join the church. Some say that is too young. I can only answer it was not too young for me. Because I then wanted to live like Jesus as nearly as I could. According to some definitions of salvation, I was not saved, but if you consider one saved who is dedicated to the best he knows, then I was saved, and so is every other person who has made a similar decision. I believe God holds one responsible only for the light he has. Thus I contend that you or your child can be saved without reading another book, hearing another sermon, or learning another truth in any way.

## Knocking at Your Door

During his reign, King Edward VIII of England was especially concerned about social conditions. He once decided to visit some of the homes in a slum section on the waterfront where he was to christen a ship. He stopped first at a house in which lived one of the most disreputable men in the area. He had become a social outcast. Hearing a knock at his door, he shouted in a gruff voice, "Who is it?"

The answer came back, "I am your king. May I come in?" Thinking it was a cruel joke, the man refused to open the door. The king, a gentleman who respected the rights of a man in his own household, would not force his way in, so he turned and left. And this poor man missed seeing his king.

John tells us that the King of kings and Lord of lords comes to the door of each of us. He says, "Behold, I stand at the door, and knock: if any man hear my voice, and open the door, I will come in to him, and will sup with him, and he with me" (Revelation 3:20). What a tragedy for one to fail to open the door!

Jesus comes knocking at our heart's door in many ways. He often knocks through our failures. Simon Peter, for example, never really opened his life to Christ until he had failed. He was too self-sufficient. But one morning, after the shameful failure of denying Christ three times, he heard the gentle knocking as Jesus quietly said, "Simon, . . . lovest thou me?" (John 21:16). Sometimes we are so proud and pleased with ourselves that we have no room for Him. Then perhaps our health fails, or we lose our possessions or our jobs, or one of our children goes astray, or our home is broken up, and we are self-sufficient no longer. Then we might hear His knocking.

He knocks through our sorrows. Many people have told me that in the midst of a deep sorrow they felt the presence and power of God in a very special way. A favorite hymn of many expresses it this way:

> *Jesus is near to comfort and cheer,*
> *Just when I need Him most.*

He knocks through our sense of inadequacy. We often become disgusted and ashamed of the life we have been living. We come to realize we are made for a better way, but our efforts to change ourselves seem hopeless and futile. Then we hear His knock as He says, "Come ye after me and I will make you. . . ." And He will make us become the better persons we really want to be.

He knocks through the lives of others. When we come in contact with some person bigger and greater than ourselves we are inspired and strengthened. It may be the gentle goodness of a mother or the manhood of a father. It may be some person we know or a great hero of history. Christ also knocks on our doors through the lives of evil and ungodly people around us. I am sure that Judas Iscariot has caused many to be loyal. When we see who has fallen, we realize that we, too, might fall, and we strive to prevent it. Isaiah heard the call of God through a realization of the needs of others. God gave Isaiah a vision of a needy, unclean world, and asked, "Whom shall I send, and who will go for us?" (*See* Isaiah 6:1–8). As Isaiah realized that he could help to meet that need, he opened his heart to the knocking.

There are other ways in which Jesus knocks: through the study of His Word, the memories of a better yesterday, the message of a church service, or the kind words of a friend. He knocks through the voice of conscience and sometimes through a special moving of His Spirit.

I was the pastor of a small church that was having a hard time raising money for missions. I announced at the morning service that I would come around that afternoon and collect the money. As I walked up the steps of one house, I saw the man inside. I knocked long and loud, but he would not open the door. He would have been glad for me to visit him, but he knew that to open the door that day would cost him something. So it is with some of us. To open our heart's door to Christ may cost us something. But to have Him is worth the cost.

## Saving

There are two reasons why we hear less in sermons today about the punishment of God for our sins than we heard a generation ago. One reason is we have come to realize that for many punishment is taken as any easy way out. A child who has been caught in some disobedience may say to his father, "All right, whip me and let's get it over with." So may a person regard the punishment of God. Very often punishment does nothing to correct the sin; it is merely salve for the conscience. As Hegel expressed it, "The sinful soul has a right to its punishment." And Plato said, "Every soul will run eagerly to its judge."

The second reason ministers today talk less about the punishment of God is that we better understand what to do about our sins. There are four main steps in dealing with sin: conviction, confession, faith, change.

1. *Conviction.* This comes not by shouting at a person about how mean he is, but rather by putting before him a vision of the better way. A social worker tried many ways to get a certain family to clean up their filthy, unhealthy house, but without success. Then one day the worker brought the loveliest potted lily he could buy and left it on their living room table. The pure lily sat in judgment upon that dirty, untidy room, causing the family to clean it up to make it a fitter place for their new possession. Then that one clean room sat in judgment on the rest of the house, so they cleaned that up, too. Jesus said, "And I, if I be lifted up from the earth, will draw all men unto me" (John 12:32). As we see Christ, "the Lily of the Valley," we realize the shabbiness of our own lives.

2. *Confession.* This means to admit the fact of our wrong without making excuses. David prayed, "I acknowledge my transgressions" (Psalms 51:3). He offered no excuses, he pleaded no mitigating circumstances. He is honest with himself and with God. Confession must be made to ourselves and to God—usually those two are enough. However, at times it helps to confess to a counselor, such as your pastor, or to a trusted friend. Almost never should confession be public.

3. *Faith.* We sing, "What can wash away my sins? Nothing but the blood of Jesus." Our faith must be in Him. The penalty of sin is separation from God. As the branch withers and dies when it is cut off from the vine, so "the soul that sinneth, it shall die" (Ezekiel 18:4). Being cut off from God, man is powerless to reunite himself with God.

The Bible tells us that Christ "ever liveth to make intercession for them [those who have sinned]" (Hebrews 7:25). The word *intercession* here means "standing between." Because Christ is God, He has hold of the power of God. Because He became man He is in reach of all men. Thus, when by faith I take Him, I become united with God. It helps to understand the meaning of the atonement of Christ when we write it "at-one-ment"—we become "at-one" with God.

4. *Change.* Becoming "at-one" with God, man is re-created. Paul says: "If any man be in Christ, he is a new creature: old things are passed away; behold, all things are become new" (2 Corinthians 5:17). The sins of yesterday are gone, "passed away," a new chance and a new life become our possession. Being a new person, we change our old ways of living and face the future with confidence, realizing "I can do all things through Christ which strengtheneth me" (Philippians 4:13). Thus we have both forgiveness and salvation.

## Hearing and Doing

Not every one that saith unto me, Lord, Lord, shall enter into the kingdom of heaven; but he that doeth the will of my Father which is in heaven.

Many will say to me in that day, Lord, Lord, have we not prophesied in thy name? and in thy name cast out devils? and in thy name done many wonderful works?

And then will I profess unto them, I never knew you: depart from me, ye that work iniquity.

> Therefore whosoever heareth these sayings of mine,
> and doeth them. . . . (Matthew 7:21–24)

The students in a theological seminary will often preach in the chapel services. Later, they will go to some of the professors for constructive criticism. Once, after giving a sermon, a certain student went to his professor to hear his comments. The professor sat silently for a time, and finally the student anxiously asked, "My sermon will do, won't it?" The professor replied, "It will do *what?*"

Sermons must say something, but also they must *do* something. In the Sermon on the Mount, Jesus set down the most important principles of the Christian faith—truths that the disciples should hear and learn well. It is important to learn, to gain knowledge, but that is never the end of the matter. There is a man nearly seventy years old who is a student in Columbia University. He has spent upwards of fifty years as a student in this university! His father had stipulated in his will that his son was to receive $300 a month as long as he was a student in college. So the man just stayed in college, taking every course that was offered. He has learned many things and has gained a number of degrees; he is probably one of the most knowledgeable men around; but, who can say that such a life is really a success? The purpose in going to school is to be able to go out in life and live the things that one has learned.

It is important to hear the truth in a sermon, but any sermon is a failure if all it does is inform. Beyond teaching the truth, the sermon should do three things: (1) It should stir our feelings. I know there are some people who feel we should leave emotion out of religion, but they are mistaken. When one hears the truth of God it should stir his heart. (2) A sermon should stimulate one's mind. We read in the Bible: "Come now, and let us reason together. . . ." (Isaiah 1:18). Without reins, the horse would run wild; and without reason and intelligent thinking, our emotions would get out of hand. But a sermon should do more than cause us to feel and to think. (3) The sermon must inspire some action. Every sermon should begin with truth and end in life.

It's good to have an emotion, but an emotion is not worth much if it does not result in action. We come away from church saying, "That was a fine service." Well, how good a service was it? Good enough to make you pay some old debt? Control a temper? Put a bridle on your tongue? Be pleasant at home? Be honest in business? Stop using profane language? Do your part in the Lord's work? It is one thing to desire the salvation of the world; it is another thing to dedicate a rightful share of your time, talent, and money to help do it.

I sometimes think that if Jesus were present in the flesh today, He might wonder why we have built such magnificent church buildings, and He might become confused by some of our intricate worship services. In a church where I was once pastor, there were two candles immediately in front of the pulpit. I did not care much for them, so one week I just took them out. The following Sunday a number of people expressed deep indignation because the candles had been removed. It appeared that, for some of them, the burning of the candles in the church was the most important activity. I think Jesus would not really care whether or not we had any candle burning in our churches. He probably would be bored listening to some of the theological debates in which Christians engage.

If Christ were here today, we may be sure that He would re-emphasize His words: "He that doeth the will of My Father." This is not to say that He would preach salvation by works—far from it. Let us emphasize the fact that we are saved through faith. Let us remember also that faith without works is dead. In the second chapter of his epistle, James felt that this was so important that he stated it three times. Certainly this is in harmony with the Spirit of Christ. Study His teachings and you will see how often He stresses the fact that those who are saved do something about it. In the story of the ten virgins, the wise virgins were admitted because they did something about the matter of oil for their lamps. In the parable of the talents, the ones who were commended were the ones who used their talents. The man who buried his talent in the ground was severely condemned. In the parable of the Good Samaritan, the priest and Levite were condemned because they simply passed by on the other side and did nothing for the wounded man. Jesus did not say, "Well *thought*, thou good and faithful servant. Thou hast heard well and thy emotions have been stirred. Enter thou into the joy of thy Lord." He said, "Well *done*, thou good and faithful servant . . ." (Matthew 25:21)

It is one thing to read the words of the Scriptures, select passages here and there, and set them up as little slogans for our lives. But it is quite a different thing to take the truths of God and spend the rest of your days trying to match those truths in your life. A lot of people think that just to speak the truths of God is enough. But the truths of God never become real for us until they become part of our actions and our lives. The Christian knows that it is not what he says, but what he *does* that counts. Someone has wisely said that if a man were to do before he got religion the things he would do if he had religion, then he would get religion. And while I believe salvation is by faith, not works, I also believe works have a lot more to do with our salvation than we realize. Works are the natural result of salvation.

## Actions Speak Louder Than Words

Two generations ago, Dr. Hugh Price Hughes was one of the great preachers of London. In that day, Charles Bradlaugh, a famous atheist, challenged the great preacher to a public debate. Hughes agreed to debate, with the following provisions: he would bring a hundred people who had been redeemed by the Spirit of Christ as witnesses to the Christian faith, and Bradlaugh was to bring a hundred pagans who had found satisfaction in their godless way of life. The hall was filled to capacity on the night of the debate. Dr. Hughes was there with his hundred people, but Bradlaugh never did show up. He could debate the preacher as long as they used arguments; but when they began using *lives*, he was defeated. As long as we simply talk to the world, we will never win, but when we begin showing the world our lives which have been redeemed by the Christ, then the world cannot argue back.

Jesus is described as One "who went about doing good . . ." (Acts 10:38). And, if we would be His followers, we, too, must go about doing good. This is vitally important, because our lives are the only "Bible" that many folks will ever read or the only "sermon" they will ever hear. The things we do and the way we live will influence others more than anything we say. One of Edgar A. Guest's poems, "Sermons We See," says it best:

> I'd rather see a sermon than hear one any day;
> I'd rather one should walk with me than merely tell
>     the way.
> The eye's a better pupil and more willing than the ear,
> Fine counsel is confusing, but example's always clear. . . .
>
> I soon can learn to do it, if you'll let me see it
>     done;

*I can watch your hands in action, but your tongue*
      *too fast may run.*
*And the lecture you deliver may be very wise and true,*
*But I'd rather get my lesson by observing what you do;*
*For I might misunderstand you and the high advice you*
      *give,*
*But there's no misunderstanding how you act and how*
      *you live. . . .*

For many years, I have felt that the most important moment in a church service was not during the anthem, or the pastoral prayer, or the offering, or even the sermon. I think the height of any church service is the final hymn. I always select that last hymn with great care. The worshipper has been inspired by the service and has heard the Word of God in the sermon. Now, during the last hymn, is the time for him to make a response, a decision, to determine a course of action. Without this commitment on the part of the worshipper, the service is in vain. So I will close this book with an appropriate hymn, and as you read the words, determine right now that you will live out your salvation every day in all that you do.

*Take my life, and let it be*
*Consecrated, Lord, to Thee;*
*Take my hands, and let them move*
*At the impulse of Thy love.*

*Take my feet, and let them be*
*Swift and beautiful for Thee;*
*Take my voice, and let me sing*
*Always, only, for my King.*

*Take my lips, and let them be*
*Filled with messages for Thee;*
*Take my silver and my gold,*
*Not a mite would I withhold.*

*Take my love, My God, I pour*
*At Thy feet its treasure store;*
*Take myself and I will be*
*Ever, only, all for Thee.*